please just F* ⌐..
it's our turn now

Born in 1980, Ryan Heath is a writer and public servant based in London. He was previously a student activist, Labor party adviser and contributor to the *Sydney Morning Herald*.

To sexy Christine,
For never telling me or the refugees to F off!*
Ryan xxx

please just F* off
it's our turn now

Holding baby boomers to account

Ryan Heath

PLUTO PRESS AUSTRALIA

First published in 2006 by
Pluto Press Australia
7 Leveson Street
North Melbourne Victoria 3051
www.plutoaustralia.com

Copyright © Ryan Heath 2006

Edited by Dennis Glover
Designed by Vivianne Douglas
Typeset by Egan-Reid Ltd, Auckland

All rights reserved. No part of this book may be reprinted or reproduced or utilised in any form or by an electronic, mechanical or other means, now known or hereafter invented, including photocopying and recording or in any information storage or retrieval system, without permission in writing from the publisher.

Australian Cataloguing in Publication Data

Heath, Ryan 1980–
    Please just F* off: it's our turn now: holding baby boomers to account

Includes index.
ISBN: 1 86403 328 2

1. Intergenerational relations – Australia. 2. Generation Y – Australia. 3. Baby boom generation – Australia. 4. Australia – Social conditions – 2001. I. Title.

305.2

Author photograph © Nick Lockett 2005

Dedication

For my mum and dad, Kerry and Ray Heath,
for always believing in me.

Contents Page

Acknowledgements   ix

Introduction   xi

PART ONE

No Label   1

1   Uber-generation   3

2   I ❤ capitalism, it's not 1968   26

3   R U talkin' 2 ME?   39

4   Secret lives of us   54

5   So we screwed up   68

PART TWO

Slouching Towards Mediocrity – Australian Under-achievement In Focus   75

6   Property apartheid and the boomer credibility gap   80

7   Generation HECS and the slow death of public education   98

8   Corporate slums   114

9   The Australian mediocracy   129

| 10 | Generation eXpat | 143 |
| 11 | Beige-town politics | 155 |

PART THREE
It's Time Boomers 173

12	The future is now	175
13	Doing It	183
14	Glue issues	200
	Conclusion	210
	Endnotes	215
	Index	229

Acknowledgements

This book has only been possible because of my privilege to meet with and discuss these ideas with so many interesting people of my generation. If this book helps put some of their ideas into the public realm where they belong then I have done my job.

I thank Tony Moore for his patient advice and both Tracey Ellery and Sarah Crisp for backing me when this book was just a flimsy *Sydney Morning Herald* column. Rebecca Huntley – you are a star for all the feedback and encouragement you have given me since my first book proposal. If amateurs are ever to be comfortable calling themselves writers they need the sort of support and feedback all of you have given.

Without implying that they endorse the book's content I would like to express my sincere thanks to the following people for their advice and time: Dennis Glover, Brendan O'Dwyer, Stephanie Peatling, Rose Tracey, Daniel Kyriacou, Anna York, Gwendolyn Carpenter, Damian Spry, Brigid Delaney, Lisa Pryor, Kate Pasterfield, Hugh Mackay, James Crabtree, Christian Ahlert, Dan Todman, Jeff Singleton, Aaron Magner, Leah Friedman, Tim Duggan, Gabi Wynhausen, Chris Hall, Chris Minns, Ben Golder, Fiona Tschaut,

PLEASE JUST F* OFF . . . IT'S OUR TURN NOW

Julia Baird, Monika Wheeler, Somali Cerise, Sunita Patradoon, Ben Smith, Tammy Ingold, Simon Moss, Daniel Brace, Bill Bowtell, Cameron Neil, Daney Faddoul, Bonnie Davies, Phil Davey, David Henderson, Rachel Hills, Tom Dawkins, Paul Bodisco, Paula Fong, Erica Lewis, Kerry Manera, Palash Dave, Scott Carn, Tim Watts, Kylie Richardson, Will Radford, Sacha Stanley, Korryn Bentley, Bernard Salt, Jo Fox, Andrew Charlton, Damian Barr, Annabel Crabb, Jane Robinson, Rannia Wannous, Simon Palagyi, Emily Mierisch, Ted McDonald-Toone, Dave Schmidt, Rina Gill, Cat Martin, Henry Parham, Andrew Green, Dion Appel, Jeremy Heimans, Toby Brennan and Daniel Pollock. Thanks to John Watts and Matthew Style for putting up with my moods, and all those people who chose to remain anonymous but whose thoughts and advice are littered throughout the text – you're in my heart and my head.

Thanks to Sandy Symons for teaching me at UTS that the mark of a good writer is not what they put in but what they leave out and to Adrian Bullock for bringing publishing to life for me at Oxford Brookes when I could easily have walked away to do other things. Any errors remaining in this work are my responsibility alone.

Introduction

Books like this shouldn't be necessary. There are better things to do than validate other people's marketing labels by talking up generational conflict. But there are also better things to do than allow Australia to believe that its 20-, 30-, or even 40-year-olds are just 'young people' unworthy of contributing to public life – mired as 'Generation Next', stuck in a queue that doesn't move, living in a generational tent city.

In today's world change happens on an unprecedented scale, yet we live in a country unable to deal with the one inevitable change we face – demographic, or generational, change. But there is no way around it, generational power is the debate we have to have.

We do degeneration, not regeneration in 21st century Australia, leaving ourselves locked in the grip of the Baby Boomer generation who rule by numbers rather than talent or potential. We value individual children more than ever but have no collective strategy for young generations. It's inefficient, unfair and dumb.

Ken Henry, Commonwealth Treasury Secretary, understands the nature of the coming problem, telling us that the ageing of the population will start to affect economic growth by 2008–9.[1] Indeed, the sixty-five and older population is likely to double by 2030. Without an overhaul Australia will face worse than the current mismatch of first-world lifestyle and second-world public culture.

While no one can say precisely what impact the demographic tide will have on Australian society over the next two decades, it is certainly clear that these matters are under-represented in all debates – from dinner tables to the nightly news. It would not be unreasonable to suggest that demographic changes will have a greater impact on people's lives in the coming years than the difference between a Liberal and Labor government. This is perhaps no different than the impact economic globalisation and technology has had on us in the previous 20 years, but it is a sobering thought indeed for anyone who believes that generations are irrelevant.

The purpose of this book is two-fold. Firstly, I want to shine a torch on the little understood group of people born after 1970, many of whom simply have to live with the silly label Generation Y at the moment. Having done that I want all readers to then lift their sights to the bigger picture and understand how those people and their attributes are useful in addressing a possible decline in Australia's standards and fortunes, if we do not make better use of our young. This book doesn't pretend to be a solution to those issues, but it demands to be seen as a start.

It is a start because it considers the means, the motive and the opportunity for change. The means is demonstrating the hidden worth of the heirs to the throne. Here you will read a sexy snapshot of my generation – the people the Boomers have kept down but not out. The motive is countering the mediocrity that is too prevalent in Australia after three decades of Boomer promises. The opportunity for change is the generational tipping point we are approaching, the successful negotiation of which will require my generation to lay its solutions and radical thinking on the table – because mere whining will not do. The conclusion is as hopeful as the demand is clear – please, please, please just fuck off – it's our turn now.

INTRODUCTION

Having lived both in and out of Australia for the past three years I know in my bones that Australia is nothing like the Lucky Country we are told it is. We no longer offer opportunity to the rest of humanity and we increasingly deny it to our own citizens. At any one time more than a million Australians live overseas in exile or because they need opportunities Australia can't or won't give them. I am often asked why I moved away from Australia and the answer is that living overseas young people get authority as well as responsibility: with your peers you can run media and government and financial markets; and you can live in genuine rather than pretend world cities. I'd rather find that in Australia, and it is horribly hard to wrench myself away at the end of every visit – but currently that's not possible.

It is my pitch to change that. This book is built on the raw sense of social justice that the Catholic school system implants in its minions. That system also tries to build communities that tame its students, but I was never brought up to 'know my place', and I have never sought to settle in one. There are too many things to fix in the world and too much fun to have while you're doing it.

Even at 11, I remember being angry at the unsafe way we were treated as primary school passengers on school buses (three to a seat and up to 120 on a single-story bus). So I organised head counts of how many were being crammed onto our buses and delivered reports to our teachers . . . until the bus company seized our bus passes and banned us. My friends and I were right to stand up to that profit-squeezing bully-boy mentality, and the fact that we didn't let being mere children stand in the way was even better. The bus company was being unjust and stupid. I wasn't asking to drive the damn bus, just for our concerns to be taken seriously. There was a better way to run that system and in management-speak it could have been 'win-win' for all involved. The burning sense of injustice I felt outside the Sawtell Primary School when our passes were confiscated remains in me today.

PLEASE JUST F* OFF . . . IT'S OUR TURN NOW

As a boy I was brought up on a news diet of Sydney's *Daily Telegraph* (at first one of two Sydney tabloids, and later the *Telegraph Mirror*) that my Dad brought home from work each afternoon. The value of the short sentence was like second nature by the time I left Coffs Harbour and collided with student politics. As a fringe activist you needed verbal punch to be listened to. Being worthy but irrelevant never cut it in adult Labor politics either (although being pragmatic and irrelevant helped!), which is where I found myself after university. So this book is accessible. If you want an academic treatise on 'yoof', then look elsewhere.

What you should expect is a book that holds Baby Boomers to account. I don't have all the answers to generational inequity – none of us do. But we won't find them unless we start looking. We hardly even know what our problems are any more thanks to years of shedding skills and refusing to ask the hard questions. Now generational inequity is a symbol of the lost dynamism required by societies destined for long-term success.

The Boomers might see themselves as permanently young and cool, but their cadre has entered its cranky conservative phase. It's time to bump these Baby Bleaters and their ceaseless cries for more milk, and their figureheads who have all the originality and sophistication of bratty two-year-olds. It's not that they don't have anything to contribute – it just shouldn't be the same contribution in the same roles as they've been giving for decades. It's time for them to move on and if they won't do it themselves those of us born after 1970 have to do it for them.

Despite their pretensions to be the embodiment of socially-just progressives, Boomers simply haven't delivered. Anne Summers wants you to write to your MP to change the world; I want you to live the change you want to see.[2] The Friends of the ABC pine for radio drama, but I pine for proper multi-channel digital TV. If you want to see apathy look to these people – they are apathetic about us.

The type of public culture currently applauded in Australia is an old person's paradise. It is familiar and slow. We have none of the chaos and public atmosphere of Asian cities, are not over-the-top like the US, lack the sheer depth of historic and emerging Europe, and have completely dropped the ball compared to the London I know and love – a place pumped full of diversity and raw opportunity. We look back and trade off a long-gone Olympics. London got theirs because the city captures the world as it is and surges forward to make what the world will be in 2012.

And in this old person's paradise – this Adelaide writ large – we have let generational change, or lack of it, creep up on us. The 1960s ended 35 years ago and it's time to get over it. Refusing to recognise that reality will see 'generational change' become 'generational conflict' in our time. Boomers can hobble away from these facts but they can't hide. It's time for open-minded people who will under-sell and over-deliver. The voices of dozens of such young people appear in these pages.

But forget the tussle of selfish generational interests for one moment and consider what it takes to make a country prosper. "Most often, groundbreaking achievements go hand in hand with youth."[3] The young achieve because they haven't learnt to follow rules and are eager to break new ground. We know how to innovate and we actually want to. Sixty-five percent of great scientists had published their most important papers by the age of 35. In 2004 a 22-year-old, Frank Wilczek, won the Nobel Prize for Physics. In 2005, 24-year-old French computer science student, Alexis Lemaire achieved the most difficult feat of mental arithmetic ever attempted by working out the 13th root of a 200-digit number – arriving at a 16-digit answer from 390 trillion possibilities in nine minutes.

Like these two talents Australia's young can take on anyone in the global marketplace. But our default position is not to embrace them, rather we let our young thinkers and doers and leaders languish in the cultural shadows in a wasteland of fringe email lists, party backrooms, websites and independent magazines, cut off from a mainstream clogged with the same old faces. Those with radical ideas and innovative ways of living, producing, and consuming rarely hit the homogenised public conversation for more than a few seconds. Few institutions reflect their values or support their innate drive.

This book is a little window into those different ways of doing things. It's not a counter-culture or a mass protest. It's not even a movement – it's a view on hundreds of little movements, technologies, communications, social networks and practical philosophies. This generation's diversity is its strength and its template for a better Australia. It's a generation that is going to change Australia because, as even Peter Costello admits, 'demography is destiny.'

So about us. We're global, responsible and live 24/7 lives. We're pro-capitalist because capitalism supports the opportunity and the lifestyle we are used to. We support social solidarity because we want a market economy without a market society. We are libertarian about personal behaviour because we believe everyone has the right to be happy. That makes us individual, not selfish: 'The self is absolutely at the centre of the iGeneration [a reference to iPods] . . . I like me. I just happen to like you too.'[4] Our consumer choices are based on personal values as well as need.[5] We are the first post-PC generation – opposed to prejudice and self-appointed cultural police alike. We've been to IKEA more often than we've been to church. We are income-rich and asset-poor, immersed in a culture of debt and the victims of 'Property Apartheid'.

We are the most educated, skilled generation yet. Our diffuse entertainment and information choices prevent us from gaining the same cultural momentum the Boomers did with their focus on traditional, obvious and public institutions like the ABC. We don't look to state power to accomplish an agenda – we're sceptical of government and would rather do it ourselves where we can. We are label-proof – the banal and generic Gen Y means nothing to any of the people I know – we've heard it all before.

INTRODUCTION

We look at life in the whole, not in little parts. We see how things relate to each other and it shows in our multi-tasking and sustainable approaches. We are not afraid to be contradictory because ours is a complex world.

The communities we make are authentic, rather than forced. Our relationships exist because of choice, not obligation. We have the integrity to show the world exactly who we are. We work in teams and eschew dull procedures and bureaucracy. We process more new information in an hour than a 15th-century peasant did in a lifetime. And, most importantly, we want to change our country.

So I want you to answer this question: do you believe the present oligarchy of leaders and cultural commissars are the people best placed to answer the questions of how to make Australia and the world a better place in 2026? Do you think progress to a society based on excellence and compassion can be achieved through lazy old critiques and cumbersome ideologies? If you agree that the old mantras of the left are impotent in the face of conservative wedge issues, join my generation in talking about the 'glue issues' that might bind us back together and move this country forward. Take the risk of letting young people drive this agenda forward.

I dream of an Australia that embraces the animated and innovative spirit of youth, not merely the buying power of suburban middle age. It's a country where companies are accountable to shareholders, consumers and the public interest. It's a country that militates against cliques and nepotism and cultivates an investment culture that rewards hard work, entrepreneurs and new ideas from whatever people of whatever age. It's a transparent meritocracy. It's long-haul Australia – relaxed and comfortable with the sacrifices and innovation needed for investing and living sustainably in this place. It's a country that rejects paternalism from every source – the state, charities and even global superpowers.

I may be of and for the intelligent Left, but this is a book for every young Australian and every older Australian who wants to leave the place in a better state than when they arrived. Boomers are particularly skilled at whining and slutting their way into society's spotlight, but the inalienable truth is that history doesn't end with them. My generation is about diversity to the nth degree – 'we can accept there are 1700 types of normal' – and this will win through in the end.[6] Our expectations are no higher than those of the generations that preceded us. We're not selfish or greedy or uncaring. If there's one word to describe us it's 'responsible'. Whether you are ready for it or not, we are going to take our turn.

PART ONE

No label

> I'VE decided that all young people should be done away with. Anyone under the age of 28.
>
> *Paul McCartney (He's 64)*[1]

> MORE than any other generation before, this one will be largely university educated, but they are destined to spend their twenties paying off student debts, their early thirties saving for a mortgage deposit and wondering how they can afford to have children. Their forties and fifties will be spent paying for their children, and their sixties wondering where the money all went.[2]
>
> *Mary O'Hara*

CHAPTER ONE

Uber-generation

'Are there such things as generations at all?' many people wonder. The answer is a resolute yes. A common cultural context affects you just as much as the religions, geography and beliefs that bind people together. Whether our parents were stockbrokers or cleaners there are certain things we share just by the accident of our birthdates. There are views and habits we hold just because of the environment we happened to be in at a particular time. To quote the writer and diarist Anais Nin: 'We don't see things as they are. We see them as we are.' Generations do exist and they matter.

There is no easy guide that sets out what generations and stages of life there are these days. As individuals we are too diverse and such an array of forces impact on our lives to believe in the simple categories that seemed to suit the 20th century. The date span of each generation shrinks as a function of the speed of change in our world; by the end of the 21st century leading Australian experts predict we'll be living between 120 and 150 years.[3] Imagine ten generations all alive at once! If that transpires there is a real risk we'll suffer from generational fatigue.

Generations are about values and shared experiences, so don't rely on shorthand dates to distinguish neatly between generations. We think of Boomers as being born between 1946 and 1961 and Generation X between 1961 and 1975, but there are many areas of overlap. Many of the subjects of the labels lived half a life before the label even became popular. You must read between the labels.

Pondering exactly how generational labels became cultural shorthand, as I watched the 60th-anniversary celebrations of the D-Day landing in 2004, it struck me that twenty-somethings in that time were a generation defined by their response to the crises of war. World War II was their ultimate shared experience. You may even have read of the American newsreader Tom Brokaw's label for them: 'The Greatest Generation'. One correspondent covering the 60th-anniversary commemorations noted the subdued atmosphere. 'This is not a generation that likes to shout its achievements from the rooftops,' he mused. Indeed, the humility of those veterans is quite awesome. And as I sat wondering if my peers would live up to their standards it was also clear how different these World War II veterans were compared to the Boomer generation that followed them. The Boomers are your classic case of salesmanship – all show. If they had a continent's liberation to celebrate you can be sure it would become a ticketed festival sponsored by a Cola company. They don't have that scenario to worry about though so they zealously guard other sacred cultural cows – like the 'peace movement' – as if they are the sole proprietors of international cooperation. That being the case, the backlash spewed out at my generation by theatre luvvie Jonathan Biggins in May 2005 is not so surprising. Biggins announced to *Sydney Morning Herald* readers that today's young have learnt nothing about war:

> No one doubts the sacrifice of the fallen, but the carefully stage-managed and art-directed dawn service [on Anzac Day] has become more about cementing in the young the idea of armed conflict as an

integral part of nationhood than a tribute to the pointless and tragic waste of every life lost on the Gallipoli peninsular.

What a dickhead. When I was 17 and making a speech for a 'Lions Youth of the Year' competition I referred to the casualties of Gallipoli as being 'lambs in a slaughterhouse'. That's why young people go to Gallipoli – they know how pointless it was. That's why they were the official marshals at the anti-Iraq street marches that Biggins presumably attended in 2003. They know that we shouldn't ever lightly tread down the path of war. They also despise simplistic nostalgia of the sort Biggins serves up. The presence of young Australians at Gallipoli each April is a quiet tirade against illegitimate power. It's a very Australian act and symbolic of my generation. But then, having spent much of their lives ignoring or denigrating Anzac Day, that's not something supposedly progressive Baby Boomers know much about.

Am I being nasty? If so, the important point is that generations differ from each other. The key question is how we measure and discuss common or destructive behaviours within and between these groups. While we can and should treat people as individuals, so we must accept and respond to documented behaviour that helps or hinders the public good. My peers are not given enough credit for the good they have to contribute to society. We hear far too little about the people of *this* century, and far too much about the Baby Boomers, the people of *last* century. And there's one fundamental thing wrong with that. You can't build the future out of nostalgia.

One word that describes us – responsible

Young Australians might have been filled with 'optimism' in the 1970s, but what summarises us now? 'Cynical' and 'apathetic' are contenders, but ultimately they're too limited and negative to ring true. We're not 'greedy' or 'selfish' either. I love cocktails and yoga and weekend city breaks, but my parents loved microwaves, washing machines and colour TV in much the same way. The point is we all like things that make our lives easier and activities that stimulate, entertain or relax us.

'Responsible' is the word that sticks best. It implies inclusiveness and communal and social attitudes. It implies our diversity will prevent us from developing any extremist momentum but it doesn't rule out having fun alongside the serious stuff. Responsible people don't rebel just because it feels good, but they know there are times and places to rebel. We should and often do live by the advice of the Kaiser Chiefs in their song *You Can Have It All*:

> Take a lesson from the ones
> who have been there/
> My brain is not damaged/
> But in need of some repair

Of course one of their other hits is called *I predict a riot*. I think there is something in that for Boomers.

So how exactly are we responsible?

Let's take illegal drugs for a start. A significant minority, sometimes upwards of 40 percent, acknowledges they take them and almost all are informed about the consequences. Nearly as many do it in moderation. For all the misplaced hysteria around tragedies like the Anna Wood 'ecstasy death' of the mid-90s it's alcohol and cigarettes that still clock up the public health bills and cause the most personal pain and suffering. Anna Wood wasn't a symbol of a lost generation, she died because she illegally went into a nightclub while underage, took way too many drugs and then didn't drink any water until it was too late.

Shift over to study and careers and you find very similar attitudes. We can't just float along '60s-style in the 21st century. Sure, young people have extraordinary opportunities – ones that didn't exist readily for groups like women until recently – but we work hard for those opportunities. And pay for them through the nose. Just look at the number of mature-age students (mostly in their twenties and thirties) heading back into tertiary education, often at night.

The evidence suggests we can be the first sustainable generation since the Industrial Revolution and what could be more responsible than being sustainable? Helped by our progressive teachers, we grew up worried about dolphins and rainforests and ecotourism. Do you think green shopping bags were last season's hit accoutrement because the blue rinse set decided to switch colours?

As we are dealing with matters natural; we can get sex anywhere, anytime, anyhow and with anyone in the 21st century. It's a freedom sanctioned by society and taken up by many. It's completely common for today's young people to have slept with 20 to 50 people and the average is rising.[4] Our sense of responsibility towards sex is detached from old notions of respectability – responsibility is not virginity, it is being safe. 'If your first experience of ten pin bowling was watching the Grim Reaper on TV kill innocent families with AIDS, you'd be careful too.'

On the other side of the condom is Daniel Donahoo, a fellow at the fledgling and youth-run think tank OzProspect who rejects the idea that we are a responsible generation. For him the 'adolescents' who avoid the risk and responsibility of moving out of home and taking on roles such as parenting in their twenties are spoiling their own lives and acting like permanent kids.[5] Where Donahoo sees irresponsibility I see a generation exercising choice.

Many young people don't want to be saddled with a mortgage or kids in their early twenties – as Donahoo was – *because* they want to be responsible. How many parents do you know who openly or secretly regretted having their kids so early? They're the ones who lock the kids in their rooms when their friends come over for a drink because they are desperate to steal back their youth. They're the ones who dump their kids home alone or in endless childcare because they weren't financially secure enough to be able to make other arrangements. That's not responsible either.

It also has to be remembered that instead of pushing our teenagers into early responsibility like full-time employment or full citizenship rights we tend now to send them off to pay for their continuing education. That's followed by a decade of finding their feet in the job market while paying their student costs back. Where's the time for parenting and mortgages with those responsibilities? So Donahoo may be right that we don't fully develop until much later these days, but that's because we've got more to develop and bills to pay for it all.

Whether you think we are responsible or not, it takes more than one word to explain a whole generation, especially one as diverse as ours.

Labels are for canned food

Generational labels are good for shorthand and nothing else.

> THERE are benefits in understanding the reasons why sets of people called Gen X or Gen Y are different from others, but it makes no sense as an individual to create an identity around those features.
>
> *Dave Schmidt, 26, Melbourne*

The harder option is investigating what people of a given age think and do, and in Australian journalism there are few people willing to make that effort and even fewer who will pay them to make it. The Baby Boomer label is well known, if uncritically accepted. There is always Generation Jones (1955–65) for those late Boomers that don't like the Boomer label. Generation X was a label for drifters with an embittered but denied sense of entitlement and removed from any actual demographic trend (arbitrarily tacked as the early

1960s to late 1970s.) Where Generation X was a flaky concept, the next set of labels is pure nonsense – none of Gen Y (how thoughtful and original), Gen Next (well, duh!) or the Millennials (could cover anyone alive in 2000, really) has stuck.

When the essence of a generation is diversity, a single label is always going to leave out the majority. Labels might work for homogenous generations, but not ours. Sydney writer Tim Duggan, 24, is certain in his assessment of his peers: 'The one distinguishing feature of my generation is its fragmentation.' Simon Moss, 22, from Melbourne says that 'we don't have one idea, we have lots of different ideas'. Scott Carn, 27, thinks it's an attitude as well as a fact: 'We can accept there are 1700 types of normal,' he says. Kate Pasterfield, 27, agrees and argues our generation is more open: 'We're not like Gen X. We don't think we know EVERYTHING. We're a lot more willing to listen and learn.'

When I think of my generation I don't think of white people going en masse to demos or apprenticeships. There is no defensiveness or irony if I start a sentence with 'Some of my best friends are ...', because some of my best friends are Thai or Bengali and work in a surprisingly long list of occupations. Reviewing the invitation list to a recent housewarming I realised my friends were journalists, teachers, artists, event organisers, clinical researchers, actors, IT support staff, bankers, flight attendants, economists, receptionists, market analysts, stylists, music producers, recruiters, production assistants, paralegals, press officers, students, archaeologists, designers, travel agents, political staffers, personal assistants, recruiters, executive officers, public servants, waiters, doctors, brokers, transport logistics coordinators, psychologists, academics, managers, website designers and union officials. That doesn't make me special, just common.

So let's forget labels and think common characteristics and situations. When that happens then we might actually start to meaningfully understand my generation, its capabilities, aspirations and flaws.

PLEASE JUST F* OFF . . . IT'S OUR TURN NOW

Fewer than 25 percent of people live in nuclear families today and, with the lock out of my generation from home ownership and the acceptance by society of open homosexuality, this number will continue to shrink.[6] As is already the case in some European countries, one-person households will soon outnumber married families with children.[7]

Headline indicators like family type now cover fewer people and tell us less about the people they do cover than in decades past. While older people tend to be obvious in their motives, style and words, people my age are far more subtle, sophisticated and varied in the way we approach and experience particular opportunities. For example, a Boomer manager will normally need to see and grip something to understand it, and they want to control. People 20 years younger are far happier for work on a project to be delivered 'just in time'; they will allow more autonomy for the people they manage and accept that feedback is a two way process. In the social sphere, as Sydney writer Lenny Ann-Low wrote about her experience of the 2005 Big Day Out (as a humble 'old' person): 'Watching the currents of Paris Hiltons chanting a Slipknot chorus . . . I realised how sophisticated these tanned waifs are compared with my years of teenage maturity-yearning.'[8] These days possessions, occupations, appearances and behaviours are not the reliable guide to other aspects of a person that yesterday's status symbols were. With us, you need to look harder.

Flexible and adaptable

> THEY (boomers) are so conservative. We are much more comfortable with change – in our time everything is changing constantly . . . computers halve in size and triple in speed within a few months.
>
> *Paula, 22, Darwin*

If diversity is our core characteristic, adapting to change is our core skill. Whereas Boomers wallow in remembrance of the good ol' days, we live change everyday, and rather like it. When we register with 'temp' agencies we cope with learning three new work systems in a fortnight; we multi-task while talking to our parents on the phone. As a representative of the International Young Professionals Foundation explained to me: 'We are comfortable with ambiguity and uncertainty. More people understand that certainty, stability and truth are probably delusions and that they probably don't exist.'

We make quick decisions and get over bad ones because complaining and over-zealous planning wastes time. The heart of this capacity is lateral thinking. And we can think laterally because our brains can think quickly – we have spent our lives processing information at a much faster rate and through more channels of communication than anyone else in history. As one rather embarrassed interview subject recalled: 'I was in the cinema watching the movie *Run Lola Run* next to a guy who was, I guess, 55. When all the fast-paced scenes were on he just couldn't understand it, couldn't process it.' We think laterally to create solutions and get around problems others try to address with formal and bureaucratic means. Our lateral thinking makes us great innovators.

The base reason for all of this isn't hard to find – it's just following a historical trend. But whereas Baby Boomers are happy to ignore that long-term trend because it suits their interests there is inevitability about the fact that for centuries our brains and our use of them have been getting better. Two recent examples of scientific studies are Harvard Medical School's study showing that older doctors have inferior knowledge to younger ones, and University of Michigan's 2001 research demonstrating that the brains of 'seniors' have to work much harder but achieve poorer results than young people on memory and mathematical tests.[9]

Today we are not only faster but more analytical. We daily reap the benefits of a longer education than our parents, one based on more than rote learning names, dates and formulas. Between 1993 and 2003 – the period in which today's under-thirties started getting qualifications, the percentage of Australians with a university or vocational degree rose from 45 percent to 55 percent.[10] And it's now well know that people with professional training have nearly 20 percent more synapses (the connections between brain cells) for each neuron (brain cell) than their less-educated counterparts.[11]

When not in formal learning our brains are still hyperactive. In his 2005 book *Everything Bad is Good for You*, Steven Johnson argues that popular culture has not dumbed society down, but skilled it up. It comes as some relief to have it confirmed that 21st century popular culture is the multi-layered and provoking experience my generation suspected it was and that experiencing it actually improves analytical and spatial skills. If you are under 35 you are almost certain to agree with this, and the chances of agreeing dwindle for every year older you are. People my age have never been the passive recipients of culture – for us it has always been a tool of learning and a way to gain understanding of the world. From my own experiences of the ancient versions of *SimCity* (a computer game teaching planning, geographic and political skills) played on the '286' computer my parents slaved to buy in 1992, to the intensely structured activities middle class parents now lock their kids into, the symptoms of our brains being programmed to take on challenges as a matter of course are everywhere. When we link these positions with solid facts such as the continuing increase in average IQ scores (accelerating in the 1990s at an annual rate of 0.36 points) there begins to appear a clear case that younger brains are holding more information and their owners, in general, do more with it than any other older group.[12] As Madeleine Bunting of *The Guardian* put it:

> Our brains are being retooled to suit an information age. A premium is put on mental speed and flexibility. Thinking fast, and absorbing and adapting new information continually is what is demanded.[13]

But in a sense how we got to be smarter and faster doesn't matter – the bottom line is we are.

So how might our brains be programmed in the future? Gwendolyn Carpenter, a 30-year-old e-government consultant, puts it best as we hunch over sushi and a laptop in a late night dive after watching the second Bridget Jones movie:

> I am part of a generation where the tools that I learn are immediately out of date. I never feel appropriately challenged. I have gotten used to being thrown into situations constantly where I have to learn to use new tools. The difference between my expectations and my parents is that I will have to continuously update. Now, it's much more important to know where to get information and how to verify it, and contextualise it, rather than to possess it. You must always be curious, and it's tiring. If you have to be constantly curious how do you do all the of the rest of the things you are supposed to do to lead a stable life.

If you are one of those people who insist on generational labels, then Gwendolyn Carpenter has summarised 'The Google Generation' perfectly. Similarly, *The Courier Mail* says we are 'hyper-qualified, technologically minded young people who have a very ambitious streak'. Meanwhile, Richard Neville, captain of the sinking Baby Boomer ship acknowledges the effect technology (discussed in more detail in Chapter Three) is having on the people who deal with it daily – us. 'It demands a higher order of mental skills, such as openness to learning, a capacity for self criticism, low defensiveness and the ability to process multiple realities and values.'[14]

And just as technology has transformed the globe it is transforming the brains that make sense of it. As a group of diverse people thinking in endless and excellent ways, it's no surprise that individuality is something we prize.

The omnipotent individual

We are the first generation who have really been allowed to be ourselves. We are networked individuals, certainly, but it's individuals, not families and communities that map our lives now. What would be tragic, however, is to let individualism degenerate into me-ism, emulating the Boomer founders of the 1980s Selfish Revolution where Gordon Gecko acolytes made greed something to be proud of. It's not. I remember enough John Donne from high school English to know no man is an island.

You can be an individual without being selfish. My friend, the British author Damian Barr says:

> The self is absolutely at the centre of the iGeneration. But we're not self-centred. We are a disparate demographic bound together by our individualism. We put on our own mask before helping others. Issues motivate us more than parties. We download singles not albums. So what if it is all about me? I like me. I just happen to like you too.[15]

I have faith in this outlook because ultimately the only way we can create a common good is by making choices as individuals to contribute to such a good. If we can't trust and encourage that individualism we can't ever achieve a wide-ranging common good. That's a very different thing from selfishness.

Being an individual is good for me and good for society. I'm much happier to rely on my outlook on the world than some artificial 'youth' culture. Spending my life chasing 'youth culture' would just be a waste of money. There are few common denominators these days, and any trend or fashion that catches-on does so for weeks or months, not seasons or years, and is replaced quickly by another. Nor is youth culture 'alternative' anymore – it is either condoned or sanitised and resold to us quicker than you can say 'charity wristbands are so 2005'.

Technology also alters our ability to commune in a youth group-think, as Boomers did, and still do. Everything from movies to shopping can all be done or experienced from home on your own these days. It's a different current altogether from the one the Boomers glided along in their Yellow Submarine.

We don't want to be like Baby Boomers

Baby Boomers are not the generation to end all generations, despite the best efforts of publications like *The Weekend Australian Magazine* to print contrary claims. To sum up WAM's April 2004 'Band me downs' article for those who fell asleep while reading it (or the 98.1 percent of you who don't buy that newspaper on a Saturday): young people sometimes like to listen to, remix or scratch around with some of their parents' Jimi Hendrix and Rolling Stones vinyls – therefore all Boomers are good.

According to the author, Deborah Cassrels, 'When teenagers start raiding their parents' record collections, and teenage bands pay homage to rock's pioneers, pop goes the generation gap.' Not convinced? To help us understand her brilliant theory Cassrels reveals that kids today are so petulant and demanding of 'different stuff' that inevitably they stumble across their parents' records and 'at the same time bridge the generation gap'. What a stroke of luck! But wait, there's more:

> ... the music has political swagger ... revolution, liberation, politicisation – are particularly enticing to young people ... (but) the counterculture is not as passionate and exclusive a concept as it was in the '60s and '70s.

Cassrels simply does not get that sampling the past is different from endorsing it. Sampling is about making old music different, new and moving it forward. Just listening to old music can bring superficial pleasure, but if that's all you ever do, you're just the victim

PLEASE JUST F* OFF . . . IT'S OUR TURN NOW

of a money-making machine exploiting your addiction to nostalgia. You are merely bringing to life the idea that 'Old rockers never die – they just tour Australia'.[16] Cassrels also exhibits symptoms of denial about the political nature of grunge, hip-hop and lots of the underground music scene. Then again, these types also think House music is something you play at auctions.

The 'Band me downs' article was published at the beginning of the week marking the tenth anniversary of Kurt Cobain's suicide. But that wasn't going to stop Glenn A. Baker chipping in to tell us about the Rolling Stones and Paul McCartney. He believes: '(their) body of work is so huge ... and had such cultural impact that younger people are in awe of it, because it's such as immense force that just comes at them.' Wrong. Fifty-six percent of 16–24-year-olds can't even recognise a photo of John Lennon.[17] What I'm truly in awe of is that Baker is so back-dated he thinks people my age would take lessons in music taste from him – a man who programs Enya and Shirley Strachan's *Christmas Children* for Qantas' in flight music system.[18]

As for the two-billion-dollar-man, Paul McCartney, he's a good symbol of all that is hopelessly conservative and conformist about the Boomers.[19] He's gone from being a sign of moral decay when he first toured America in the 1960s to being the $6,000 a second family-friendly alternative to Janet Jackson at the Superbowl. It's no surprise that the most lucrative song for this new Bing Crosby is *Yesterday*.[20] And expect to see him back for the next Live 8 in 20 years time where he's sure to be a young 83.[21] He's 64 in 2006, and guess what – we don't need him. Never mind Ringo Starr who is now developing a franchise in which he will play an animated superhero version of himself who is 'an evil-battling, earth-saving superhero with a great sense of rhythm' (and let's not start on the 'fashion' label Eric Clapton just launched, aged 57). There is such a lack of irony in these actions that I am increasingly glad I chose to use my hardcover copy of McCartney's biography as a doorstop.

UBER-GENERATION

Ten differences between People of this Century and People of Last Century

1. We are the most diverse and socially-inclusive generation ever.
2. We are sophisticated and contradictory rather than obvious and homogenous in our tastes.
3. We are flexible, resilient and can multi-task well.
4. The majority of us are tertiary educated, no other generation is.
5. We are the best-travelled generation and have international networks and relationships not based on proximity.
6. We are income-rich but asset-poor, older generations have more assets proportionally.
7. We are a user-pays generation, our lives are ruled by debt.
8. The boundaries between our personal and professional lives are blurred, as is the case between our genetic families and new urban 'families' based on friendship.
9. We place our single or multiple individual identities at the core of our being, and offer ourselves to a collective will on a case-by-case basis.
10. We prefer to be understated: promising little and delivering more than expected.

But they go on: 'All you can really be now is a good pastiche artist.' (Translation – sorry, kiddies, you're all crap). 'To boomers, even relatively new bands such as The Darkness, Coldplay, The Strokes, Jet, The Vines and White Stripes are echoes of the past.' I noted the absence of Scissor Sisters, Franz Ferdinand, The Streets, Ben Lee, Missy Higgins and Maroon 5 from that list (and more recently the likes of Goldfrapp, The Magic Numbers and Kaiser Chiefs) – which shows that pop tarts Baker and Cassrels aren't exactly 'with it'.

And we don't care about the world? Bollocks. What about the Black Eyed Peas' 2003 political anthem *Where is the Love?* A

A day in my life

Over a three-month test I sent an average of 51 work emails and 10 personal emails a day (or six for each hour in the office). I make 20 to 30 phone calls each day, and send an average of eight text messages. My personal communications are dominated by text and work by email. When I tested the reactions of Baby Boomers to these figures their responses fell into two categories: disbelief that anyone could waste so much time communicating like this or insistence that, having observed my life, the real figures must be higher.

Work for me is about delivering many things 'just in time'. It is not about linear progress on a project or working the hierarchical system. My days are a sea of chaos, and success is often defined by keeping my head just above water. But I enjoy the adrenalin buzz and solving problems fast. There is no time for valuable reflection or self publicity. When I do succeed it is because of the relationships and networks I have developed – a team effort saving the day. Here is a typical chronology.

0700 Wake up (did I really drink that last glass of wine?).
0720 Really wake up after pressing snooze twice.
0730 Shower (city living just ruins your skin – moisturising essential).
0745 Fresh coffee and toast (OK, so usually I'm late and get McDonalds).
0800 Bus, then train to work. If not rushed then walk part of the way and get a nice coffee and bagel.
0845 Start work: catch up on email (usually 20 unfinished emails at any one time), delegate tasks, attend meetings, make site visits, brief boss, anticipate and make decisions for boss etc . . .
1345 Realise I have missed lunch and get snack, or eat sandwiches in a working lunch meeting.

UBER-GENERATION

1400 Have flicked through papers for work, try to spend an hour focusing on a major task that is slipping.

1600 Have been interrupted by a serial loiterer hanging around my work cubicle and taken four phone calls in 15 minutes. Put phone on divert and cite 'urgent ministerial meeting' to any important people who have been sent to voicemail.

1601 Fed up – need fresh air and a newspaper break for 10 minutes. Stupidly spend $5 on fresh juice at convenience store.

1800 Go for a swim at my gym (ok, so I spend half the time in the spa). Ignore all gym equipment – of course – using time pressure as excuse and pray my high metabolism lasts until I'm 30.

1930 Finish up some bits at work and rush so I'm not too late to networking event (ninety percent wankers – scour for vaguely interesting company then leave). Write up overtime sheet – average three hours a day.

2015 Head to pub dinner (the preferred event for the evening), apologising for yet again prioritising work over friends.

2030 Pointless work call reminds me of why I am stressed. Remind self to spend all that overtime money on a decent massage. Fail to acknowledge irony of this.

2031 Wonder why I am still single.

2130 Take train home.

2230 Realise I was actually an hour later getting home than I thought (cite urgent third bottle of wine).

2245 Make dinner if haven't eaten or make some calls to family and friends.

2300 Bath soak, pay TV, reading, personal emailing or doing 'to do' list for work.

0030 Head to bed, try to have chamomile tea to help get to sleep.

0045 Tea is useless – take herbal sleep remedy.

PLEASE JUST F* OFF . . . IT'S OUR TURN NOW

worldwide smash with an anti-war message: 'Can you practise what you preach/Where is the love?' And PS, the LA-based front man from Black Eyed Peas is so outraged at the lack of innovation and risk-taking in the Australian music scene that he is moving to Sydney for six months a year to sign up all the talented acts currently ignored by our record labels. Back to our politics – spare a thought for the 2004 resurrection of Band Aid by Coldplay's Chris Martin before Bob Geldof decided to re-hog centre stage for Live8. Chris Martin kick-started the reinvigoration and with a lot less bluster that Geldof. I wish the Boomer nay-sayers had been there as my office stopped work to listen to the first airing of the Christmas 2004 *Feed the world* before going out to buy copies. The participants were a lot younger and far more diverse than the recycled do-gooders who headlined at Live 8 in July 2005 (worthy though they were).

Another thing I can't stand is the earnestness with which Boomers enjoy their music – there's not a hint of irony. Goldie Lookin' Chain's *Guns don't kill people, rappers do* would never have got a look-in with this lot in the 1960s. More topically, why was a single column inch devoted to the 40th anniversary of the 1964 Beatles tour of Australia in 2004? Anniversary coverage is lazy and self-indulgent – cross-promotion and spin dressed up as history. I have never sat around lighting candles in memory of my first Roxette tape. My suggestion to all those interviewed is: go find your dignity. But given the immense money-spinning popularity of the 'heritage acts' of rock and pop who pack out stadiums with soccer mums and sugar daddies, no one is likely to take my advice soon. What I find sad is that both the performers and audience are like the sort of person that really enjoys a school reunion. Even cosmetic surgery is less pathetic than these mass acts of denial. The therapy bills are not worth thinking about!

And so our culture lives with the belief that because one (and only one) generation of people could find no better way to define themselves than through mildly talented American folk singers and Liverpudlian pretty boys, that music must somehow abandon its historical role as distraction and uplifting spectacle in order to serve the needs of that generation. Where are the new Beatles? Big news: there aren't ever going to be any 'new Beatles' because we all have better things to do with our lives now. It's like complaining that horse-drawn coaches just aren't what they used to be. My generation has great non-musical ways to express our values and there is nothing wrong with that.

Spoiled by choice

Choice is important to us. Without choice you cannot be an individual, nor can you be independent. But choice can also make one's life worse – to the point where some enterprising kids have even managed to write a book about the 'Quarterlife Crisis' that too much choice supposedly generates.

Sydneysiders Rachel Hills and Kate Pasterfield, told me in separate interviews that choice can 'paralyse you'. According to David, 27, from Melbourne, 'You end up just going to the first tangible things you see. You trust word of mouth, because dealing with all the choices is stressful.' The son of a teacher confided to me that his mother despairs at what teenage boys go through when planning life after school:

> She says there are boys who are just so overwhelmed by the opportunities that are available to them that they don't know what to do. They say "dunno, miss, dunno". They end up getting drawn to really misleading courses of study – things like business and marketing – because they're Mickey mouse subjects that seem relevant but don't force you to confront any issues.

Too much choice is the opposite of what other 20th-century generations were subjected to.

PLEASE JUST F* OFF . . . IT'S OUR TURN NOW

> IT seems that things were so much simpler for our parents – everything was defined. You had a few options but, generally, you got a job, got married and did it for life. People our age are bewildered by choice.
>
> *Sacha, 25, Perth*

Enjoying choice presupposes that you have the time and energy to do so. I often find myself blocking exciting and interesting choices out of my mind. I order latte without thinking, because it hurts to think. I don't want the choice making process to ruin the result.

Take the skin-care and hair-care sections of a large supermarket, for example. It's always the super pretty products that make claims about being 'revolutionary' and 'ground-breaking' that completely bugger me up when shopping. And I always waste money on this stuff because I think it will relax me. But, in fact, the opposite is happening. You can spend half an hour comparing shampoos and conditioners – 89 choices I counted in one Sydney supermarket. Does anyone even know what 'Hydratein' is? And how will it help my hair? And what about when choosing between 20 different mobile phone plans with 10 different companies available on 42 phone models? What about when the Internet isn't fun anymore because you can't remember whether Company X wants a four-word, six-word, or eight-word password? Is it meant to be just Alpha-Numerical or Alpha-numerical, with a change of caps? Does it just want a password or both a user-name and a password? Will I have to change it after 30 days, not using any of the previous 12 passwords? And then only to buy a ticket to the summer outdoor cinema!

Now I don't want to sound 'anti-choice'. My generation is overwhelmed by choice as consumers – but not as citizens. When it comes to public culture – like media, politics, education and ways of working – things remain monolithic and rigid. Too much consumer choice about mobile phone plans and shoes is paralysing, but more choice in fundamentals, like sources of information and political parties and policies, is needed. My generation needs to move beyond the consumer clutter that paralyses us, and direct our love of choice to things that really matter.

The effect of mass travel and global information

> As well-travelled, technologically literate citizens our engagement with and interest in the world is arguably the strongest of any generation in history.[22]

Global trade accounts for around 30 percent of world GDP – four times its share in the early 1970s.[23] The massive worldwide coverage and interest in the US political conventions in 2004 drove home the point that the exhilarating dynamics of globalisation are spreading to democratic politics as well as capitalist economics. Today around half of Australians under 30 have travelled overseas in the past year.[24] If you can save an airfare, it can be cheaper to mingle in South-East Asia than spend your summer break in Australia.

In this environment we are never going to make the same choices at the same time or even be guided by the same values as Boomers. Few young people today are happy to accept the role and inevitability of our oldest institutions in affecting our lives. Only a minority look to our national government as a source and force of good in the world. Not particularly because of the Howard Government itself; it's mostly a reflection on the powerful global influences on our lives.

Our views don't come from our parents, and sometimes not even our teachers. We use visual stimuli as diverse as 24-hour international news channels, Google and global brands. Twenty-nine-year-old Canberran Cameron Neil, thinks that a childhood of stimulation has engendered our need for speed. He tells in a phone interview set up after I put a call out on a youth email list: 'Growing up with instantaneous access to information ... we're not prepared to sit around and wait for things. There's an instant gratification thing that permeates a lot of what I see.'

While Baby Boomers might have worried about a nuclear holocaust, we had that and other nightmares packed into the wee hours. A primary school project stored in my parents' garage called '2050' expresses outrage at AIDS and worries about global warming. It sat on top of my donation record sheet for a '40-Hour Famine'. Yet at the same time our experience of direct and personal hardship is so different and limited that we can't help but take a different perspective to mass tragedy. September 11 and the Asian Tsunami are horrific but removed experiences – their scale and impact prove how global our existence is yet few of us have suffered even indirectly from them. Fewer people died because of political violence (i.e. war) in 2003 – some 27,000 – than at any time since the 1920s.

All the while, successive national governments have redefined what it is to be young. The privileges of full employment, free education and welfare without means tests are now replaced by systems of debt and dependence that keep many attached to the family home until their early thirties. Yet whatever the frustrations at the mean-spiritedness of the national government, our awareness of our relative privilege is a greater influence:

> WHEN you travel everywhere, you realise how good we have it. It's hard to come back and be passionate about the fine points of domestic service delivery and state politics. It takes the edge off it.
>
> *Aaron, 32, Sydney*

We want to be part of something bigger than our families, our local community and our nation. We don't suffer from any cultural cringe, but nor are we foolish enough to be satisfied with what our country alone has to offer. For us, the greatest show is Earth.

Common threads

Given I don't own an opinion polling company and you will need to pay between $10,000 and $20,000 for access to the only substantive research into Gen Y lifestyles, there are a few things I do have to rely on others for.[25] And I do feel sad for having to rely on the Australian Democrats 2004 youth poll to tell me about what young Australians have in common. However, no one else is asking us about anything except iPods and Paris Hilton, so there is little choice. And while precocious school representatives are probably over-represented in the sample, 1200 people can't all be wrong. Here's what those people said:

- half knew someone who had attempted or committed suicide
- 70 percent did volunteer work
- 70 percent said the Federal Government's 25 percent rise in HECS fees would put them off university
- 75 percent favoured the direct election republican model
- 40 percent of those eligible to enrol to vote had not done so
- only six percent trusted politicians and seven percent trusted the media.

Other international polls suggest more than three-quarters of 16-year-olds have friends of a different race; most have gay friends; and barely any still consider certain occupations suitable only for either men or women, while they overwhelmingly prefer working excessive hours for high pay, rather than having work/life balance. Only 23 percent supported the war in Iraq.[26] Surveys show about three-quarters of young Westerners are interested in public affairs but less than half are interested in party politics.[27]

All these anecdotes and traits point to a generation capable of making the clichéd 'difference' to our world. We have the capability and the instinct to be leaders of lasting change – to my great relief I won't have to rely on the Australian Democrats for that.

CHAPTER TWO

I ♥ capitalism, it's not 1968

Why am I a capitalist?

Today, if you care about other people, capitalism is the only game in town. Sure, there's biffo in this game, and not everyone plays by the rules, but at least you're allowed on the pitch and you have a chance to prove yourself. You can travel anywhere on Earth, including the capitalist theme park that is China, and find this to be the case. And because we do travel everywhere we know it to be the case in the most tangible sense.

The title page of Naomi Klein's *No Logo* reads: 'NO SPACE. NO CHOICE. NO JOBS. NO LOGO.' (Followed by the logo of Flamingo, her publisher). Peer through the beautiful reportage and it's hard to see how the critique allows any form of alternative to the capitalism my generation has come to accept, if not love. For the first time ever capitalism is now a global economic system and my generation is the first global generation. Capitalism makes sense in our world. Just as liberal democracy is the most scalable of political systems, capitalism is the most scalable economic one. In our flexible, hyperactive world any system that isn't scalable is doomed to failure. But we shouldn't live with capitalism just because it's there. We can improve it and the society that surrounds it. Change is no threat to capitalism, it is its lifeblood.

We expect more from capitalism than anyone else – so we are going to force it to work less corruptly, more ethically and to deliver more choices to us than anyone else has been able to so far. Perhaps more than anything else, my generation can re-inject the value of trust back into capitalism, and, after that, back into our democracy. We're doing it already on the Internet – millions of chat and trade communities exist based on relationships that have never been consummated in real life, technologies such as Skype – voice over the Internet software that allows free calls to anywhere in the world – are junking whole unnecessary capitalist industries (in this case fixed line telephony). These ventures combine risk and trust in the most dynamic ways. They are the antithesis of all those electronic ticket gates at train stations that scream: we don't trust you. The antithesis of all those signs about the right of shop staff to check your bags that scream: you're a shoplifter until proven innocent. Those risk averse systems deny the reality that capitalism only works when people trust each other to part with money, just as politics only works when the public trusts politicians. Just as societies only work when young people are trusted with authority.

The sustainable generation

A global outlook goes hand in hand with believing in sustainability. If you have one you have the other because both inherently accept that the world in interconnected.

I get excited every time I walk past the 'Red Building' at the University of New South Wales in Sydney's Kensington, a suburb wedged between the city's industrial fringes and glamorous eastern beaches. As you thread your way through the campus you come upon it via a grand forecourt quite like a European plaza. More importantly, as the sun beats down on the cosmopolitan student

PLEASE JUST F* OFF . . . IT'S OUR TURN NOW

crowd the building is also enjoying the sun. The building is using the sun to be completely self-sufficient. It excites me, but it doesn't surprise me. In a way it's part of me – like a sustainability gene.

Huh? Yes, a sustainability gene – and the reasons for its existence are a John Howard nightmare of bed-wetting proportions. It's because I've been surrounded by environmental propaganda from a young age. The fervour of a competition my class entered in Year 5 to see which school could recycle the most is one I remember fondly. I was very worried about animal extinctions and acid rain in Year 6 – and would yell at the TV when *The Comedy Company* lampooned scientists warning us about global warming. I still want to slap people when I see them watering their gardens in the morning (anyone who has grown up with water restrictions knows that the sun will cause the water to evaporate before it's any use and you'll just have to do it again in the evening, dammit!).

Thinking about the environment is not a fad, luxury, afterthought or something to be expressed through the purchase of Planet Ark Washing Powder (which is good – try it). It is just something we have grown up with. And because we think about the environment intrinsically we are likely to be the generation that makes sustainability a reality in the post-industrialised West.

Givers not takers

It's predictable then that a sustainable generation is a generous generation. We don't talk the talk without walking the walk when it comes to helping others – we are made of sterner, responsible stuff. Research shows we give to causes in a far more substantial way than other generations. Young people's giving is weighted toward medical research and care (35 percent), helping children and young adults (19 percent) and people in developing countries (17 percent). Less than one percent goes to religion.[1]

The point about religion is telling. In the early 1990s I vividly remember local Catholics pressuring my mother to stop a World Vision child sponsorship she had going through our church 'Family Group'. Essentially this was an exercise that cost each of these families two dollars a month. They told her that charity begins at home. That made me sick and it still makes be baulk at authority. The group of families still works together to support each other and do good things, conveniently ignoring the fact my parents haven't set foot in a church in 15 years and wholeheartedly support their gay son. But that is the story of the modern Catholic Church and countless other institutions. And that's why you have to look past the obvious to get to the truth about how generous my generation is – because we give in different ways to the conventional church plate, telethon or demo-bucket.

More often than not young people are time-rich and idealistic. This is reflected in the increasing hours being spent on volunteering across Australia – and makes the point that we recognise that our time and talents are more valuable gifts than our money. The 2004 Australian Democrats Youth Poll I cited in the previous chapter found that 70 percent of 15- to 20-year-olds spent time volunteering. Meanwhile, busy young people are breaking ground in other ways. Good Company is a group of young professionals who donate their skills to charities. According to one member, Warren Lee, 'It's not that they (young people) are mean-spirited, but their pattern of contribution is very different . . . they don't just want to hand over a cheque. They want to become involved and have an enriching experience.' As reported in the *Sydney Morning Herald*, Good Company has 1000 members who do everything from painting shelter sheds to designing websites free of charge. Programs for donating money from one's pay packet are also highly popular amongst young people.[2]

It's not young people who are apathetic, but the older people who make this false claim. They are more apathetic in a general sense and apathetic about engaging with the truth about young people.

PLEASE JUST F* OFF . . . IT'S OUR TURN NOW

21st century activism

The nonsense view that today's young people are not as passionate, numerous or talented in their activism as the 1960s and '70s generations deserves a good kicking.

One only had to cast a glance at the audiences of the Live8 concerts in July 2005 to see that the apathetic stereotype is a myth. Look back at those front pages, at the souvenir DVD, at your own memories, and you will see them awash with youth. Look back at the message and the tactics and compare them to the failed simplicity of 20 years earlier. No one can doubt the idealism and passion of the original Live Aid, but it was charity and it was not the answer. Both the people of Africa and we learned that the hard way in the intervening 20 years. We are a generation that has moved on, become more sophisticated, and retained the passion to make the world a just and better place.

Committees and clunky institutions beloved of older generations are no longer the agents of political activism. Parliaments and bosses are not always useful or relevant targets for political action, and every year a new technology gives us a different way to spread a message. It's bonkers to think the organising methods of 1968 cut ice today. We're dealing with a new politics just as radical as the late 1960s and early 1970s, only this time it won't be televised.

There is now a stigma of pointlessness about mass street protests – those snake-like symbols of the Boomer generation. For sure we can never really know the full impact of a social movement even at its height – these things change attitudes and minds for a lifetime in some cases and they take time to bear fruit – but it seems likely the anti-corporate globalisation and anti-Iraq protests have failed to deliver anything more than temporary zest to activist circles, student life and some Boomer nostalgia. Who really gives a damn about a sit-in or 'occupation' today? Is there a university administration or well-oiled corporate PR team that doesn't know they will successfully resist protesters demands with some clever 'key messages' and stalling tactics? Do you even stop to yawn anymore at the latest ragtag group of protesters marching down that single lane of whatever CBD street leads to their state parliament? The truth is that even when massive and inspiring protests numbering up to 300,000 a city took place in 2003, Government policy on Iraq just got smarter and nastier. That doesn't make a street protest pointless, but it should make you question its relative merits.

My own moment of realisation came in August 2000 at a student National Day of Action I had been working to organise. The turnout was embarrassing. The usual 1500 chanters and banner bearers were a sad rump of 50. We were forced onto the pavement because the police could not justify closing off a lane for our funereal procession from Sydney's University of Technology to its Town Hall. As we were herded up the gutter into the malevolently apathetic shoppers, a bus passed us. I turned to my friend and fellow activist Somali Cerise and lamented 'there's more people on that bus'. She laughed, but it was a sad moment.

Enough is enough! However sad it is, we're too smart to follow the advice of the American 1960s radical Todd Gitlin. In a patronising letter to young 21st-century activists he advised: 'Be original. See what happens.'[3] Of course, if only we'd thought of that earlier! (Never mind that what he means is do exactly what people did in 1968). But seriously, it's a lovely sentiment, and probably useful to the privileged white kids of his generation who got to sit around and contemplate their henna-tattooed navels while other people fought the Vietnam war and fulfilled their social role of manual labour rather than university study. But today the public audience for activism is bored and the police are experts at clamping down on physical protest. Next time you wish 'the students' would add a bit more 'colour' to the evening news, spare a thought for the 'facts'.

We need to be original but being original isn't enough. Let's look at the practicalities of protest in the age of terror. Looking back at the anti-Apartheid movement, for instance, activists stormed the Sydney

PLEASE JUST F* OFF . . . IT'S OUR TURN NOW

Differences between Boomer activism and activism of this century

Ann Summers' 10 most stupid ways not to achieve anything:

(actually titled *Ten ways to change the world* from www.annsummers.com.au)

1 *Write the prime minister a letter* (not an email, a letter).
2 Find out who your *federal member of parliament* is and send her/him an email.
3 Choose one of your *senators* and email her/him as well.
4 Make sure the *women members of parliament* know how you feel.
5 Join one of the *political parties* and work to achieve change from the inside.
6 Write a letter to the paper to express your views.
7 Ring up talkback radio and air your opinion.
8 Check out the *groups* that fight for women's equality.
9 Boycott companies that are unfair to women.
10 Above all, talk about this stuff. Share your thoughts and feelings with your friends, people at work, your family, anyone you come in contact with.

Ryan's suggestions for achieving lasting social change:

1 Choose an education and career path that is meaningful to you.
2 Agitate and make changes in your immediate environment – be a better line manager at work, change your household's environmental approach.
3 Get plugged in – make sure you have access to the information that will keep you up to date on news and developments on the issues and values that matter to you.
4 Vote and campaign around elections – this is when politicians and citizens pay most attention to political issues.

I ♥ CAPITALISM, IT'S NOT 1968

5. Be an ethical consumer and a socially responsible investor – buying organic and buying shares that don't fund companies selling arms to child soldiers is not that hard!
6. Don't waste your time writing a letter or email to an MP unless you have a plan to follow it through or are making a tailored contribution to an organised campaign. All the other correspondence is chucked out or they use your details to send you junk mail about how important they are.
7. Actively support organisations that share your values – donate money, buy their publications, share them with your friends – activism is not a dirty word.
8. Learn how to articulate that politics is what happens in your daily life and spread this message.
9. Pay attention in school or university to citizenship education. If you're past all that, make an effort to do a short course on it or buy a book about our political system.
10. Volunteer your time if you have any spare. Time is so much more important than money to some groups, so being time-rich but cash-poor actually means you can make more of a difference.

Cricket Ground during a Springbok v Wallabies test match in order to saw down the wooden goal posts. Do you seriously believe anyone could smuggle hacksaws into the Sydney Cricket Ground today?

Having had quite big guns pointed at me close-up and personal by the NSW Constabulary at a peaceful protest attended by a dozen people in 2001, I've seen police over-reaction first hand. It's quite stupid that a little flag I was carrying could trigger what, at that time, was Australia's biggest anti-terrorist mobilisation since the Hilton bombing.[4] When those boys from Sydney's exclusive Trinity school were found guilty of raping their schoolmates with a wooden dildo, I was incredulous to discover they got a lighter punishment than a group, including me, got for peacefully protesting against the introduction of the GST at the NSW headquarters of the Australian Democrats in 1999 (a three-year good behaviour bond, as it happens). The lesson: life is not like it used to be for activists.

The US has just doubled the funding of its non-lethal weapons program. Mega-megaphones reaching 150 decibels over a 300 meter radius are being deployed to disperse crowds following trials in Iraq. Malodorant balls (high-concentrate stink bombs) have been invented for use in paintball type guns while 'active denial technology' that uses microwaves to debilitate the sense of touch is already being used on US warships.[5]

Yet despite this context more of today's under-thirties have participated in demonstrations than the equivalent group in 1974 — it's just that society gives neither credit nor respect to their activism. So the challenge is not to interest young people — they already are interested. The real challenge is to re-invent activism that is actually effective for new times, and that is something my generation is rather good at.

Examples of my generation in action

My generation is populated by strong and professional individuals with resilience, ideas and critical capabilities. These are a better basis for collective action than the amateur and dutiful drones so common in older political circles.

Simon Moss is an undergraduate student at the University of Melbourne and is involved in The Oaktree Foundation. Sylvie Ellsmore first approached me to support what is now Reconcili-ACTION in March 2002, a partnership between indigenous and non-indigenous young people breathing new life back into old aspirations. Simon says:

> Our vision (for the Oaktree Foundation) is of young people learning through partnership; young people in the developed world using and

expanding their knowledge and skills to help young people in the developing world gain access to quality education.'[6] All the people are under 25 and the emphasis is getting away from the bureaucratic model. We help young people with an idea to just go out and do it. Older people spend so much time talking. We don't have this perception that you have a skill set that's narrow. Everyone can do everything with a bit of help – their skills are interchangeable. Young people today tend to say 'never done that before, but give me 10 minutes'. They are certain there is a way to achieve things.

For the members of ReconciliACTION, the shoes of Ted Noffs, Charles Perkins and Jim Spigelman are big to fill. Whether it's reimagining the 1965 Freedom Rides for their 40th anniversary – to embed change rather than highlight injustice – or organising writing competitions for schoolkids, ReconciliACTION emulates and out-does the 'Freedom Riders'. It's not white people relieving guilt, either. Around half of ReconciliACTION's members are Indigenous and half are non-Indigenous. According to the group's website (**www.reconciliaction.org.au**) their name reflects the belief that Reconciliation has to be about more than words.

The state

You might have noticed that The Oaktree Foundation and ReconciliACTION are not government initiatives. It's no coincidence. Whereas previous generations might have waited for International Year of Youth or relied on government programmes to provide a youth activism platform, we were not brought up to have implicit trust in the state or believe in 'big government'. Questionable state power concerns us as much as reckless multinationals.[7] From our perspective, saying you believe in big government is like saying you believe in purple cars. Neither statement is very smart. Both government and cars are only fit for certain purposes – and whether they are big or purple is irrelevant – the question is: are they fit for the purpose at hand?

The fact that our first experiences of public enterprise were a series of state government bankruptcies and the raising of education fees while other taxes were slashed, affects our view of the state. When the 'left', as the obvious supporter of a reinvigorated state, can do little more than support a 'welfare equivalent of Fordist mass production' where good government equals more welfare cheques, we've had little to inspire a different view.[8] Crucially, the private sector has spent decades plying us with choice, luxury, entertainment and ceaseless fantastical advertising about itself, and government has never caught up.

The legacy of government in my developing mind was the cultural mindset Hawke and Keating created for Australia. It was not about what government could tangibly deliver but about how government made you think. In 2005 government does not make us think at all. And when it comes to delivery I, like much of my generation, have moved on. While there are some things we do want the state to do for us, most of the time we'd simply like it to enable us to do things for ourselves – in our own time, at our own pace. We don't so much need services and hand-outs as we need choices. We get more choices if we have accurate information, competitive markets and devolved decision-making. We might see Government as a catalyst for solutions, but not often as the solution itself. Indeed we are not afraid at all to question whether it is even legitimate. We can ask those questions because we have moved beyond concepts like left and right, socialism and two-party politics. What is replacing those concepts are more sophisticated and trans-partisan world views. We can see the merits of particular ideological points but are not prepared to be limited by them. Yet there is a dark demographic cloud trying to limit us and government. It's a generation – the Boomers – preparing to demand endless resources to fund their ageing. Now the people who must fund the bulk of

I ♥ CAPITALISM, IT'S NOT 1968

those demands – those born after 1970 – are increasingly suspicious of both government and the ageing people in control of it. Do you see where the clash might come from?

We defer to no one

Nothing sums up this generation's attitude to stardom and authority better than my favourite band – the Scissor Sisters. Or as the strapline for their first DVD goes – 'We Are Scissor Sisters . . . And So Are You'. Today's bands don't just play at you or for you – music fans, like any decent publication's readership, are now much more part of the creative process.

This is a generation that defers to no one, a group that has been identified by some marketing companies as 'The Challengers'. We don't like hierarchies and we don't like people who expect something for nothing. Respect is a privilege not an entitlement. Women certainly do not defer to men anymore. There is still intolerable and systematic homophobia in our playgrounds but you'd be hard pressed to find it in workplaces or social networks where young adults have a strong presence. Macho is on the way out at a serious speed. It's the evidence of a genuinely progressive generation getting to grips with itself – a victory for ideas and facials.

Everything is fair game these days, from celebrities to TV scripts. All are to be dissected and mimicked and mashed-up with what level of irony seems appropriate for the situation at hand. We'll talk through movies and *Desperate Housewives* and it doesn't disturb us one bit – it's what watching these shows is about. We are not spectators – they are interactive experiences.

And because this post-modern 'experience' is so common we won't even remember it next year, let alone in four decades. There will be no official version of the 1990s, unlike the 1960s, because few things stand out anymore, and we all experienced it differently.

Our refusal to defer is the product of not being able to rely on most people and institutions. People my age have, at some point, experienced the bitter realisation that unlike the indulged generation before us, we have to rely on ourselves. Maybe you spent your childhood dodging church paedophiles, or maybe you are just like 'Emma' in the ABC documentary *Growing Up Fast* – 'I don't think anything that I've ever done or will do in my life will be as easy as what it has been for my parents.' Whatever the case there is no easy leg up for us.

Carrie Bradshaw says in *Sex and the City*: 'All we can do is play the hand we've been given and accessorise the outfit we've got.' While you might think Carrie's IQ is smaller than her Manolo's she is right in that today we must jostle with people from every culture and continent when seeking cultural attention. In the 21st century standards are higher and the competition is cut-throat. The lazy, exclusionary economy of 1960s and 1970s Australia is gone. So we can't afford to defer out of 'respect', we can't pretend our world is different to what it is. We just have to keep the attitude and accessorise the outfit we've got. But that's OK. It's sexy, it's versatile and so are we.

CHAPTER THREE

R U talkin' 2 ME?

Within an hour of the first bombs exploding in July 2005, deep under the maze of central London's underground train system, I was bombarded with emails and text messages from friends on both sides of the world. All the while my broadband-less parents sweetly but obliviously toiled away at an email of their own (about cousins and siblings and weather; over capitalised, no spaces between words, no paragraphs, no sense of email style . . . you know the drill) clogging the phone line. I watched *Sky News* show my workplace as a potential target for the next wave of bombs that never came and was evacuated from the building before making any contact with my parents, hoping my friends had the sense to pass on my messages in case anything did happen, making contact only after walking home for two hours in the rain. That day was also the day of the citizen reporters – the images you remember were captured by ordinary Londoners thrown into chaos on their way to work. Nothing tops that day as a demonstration of how technology and communications have changed lives compared to decades past; what it improves and what it can never replace.

The bloggers that coordinated the first rescue efforts after the

PLEASE JUST F* OFF . . . IT'S OUR TURN NOW

South Asian tsunami in 2004 will tell you the same thing; even the Vatican officially communicated the Pope's death to the outside world via a Crackberry. That's Blackberry for the non-obsessed, and a cross between a computer and a phone for the uninitiated.[1] Across the board new technologies are re-shaping our lives, providing the formative experiences and becoming the tools of today's young.

All this would be irrelevant to a generational discussion except that this world is inescapably different from the world in which my parents grew up. When my parents were in their twenties a billion Chinese lived in grinding poverty – now I can call 335 million of them on my mobile phone. 640k 'ought to be enough for anybody,' said Bill Gates in 1981, but now that's not even enough memory to save a good quality photo from last night's party.[2] Now IBM's Blue Gene computer can perform 70.72 trillion calculations a second, and even a PlayStation has one percent of the power of the human brain.[3] In the US you can now purchase disposable video cameras that weigh less than 140 grams, for $AU40.[4]

Up until 1980, when I was born, there were only three communications technologies of note that had any mass application – radio, terrestrial TV and the fixed telephone. Look at what we've seen since then – VCR, DVD, mobile phone, Internet, satellite/cable TV, CDs, personal computers, Voice Over the Internet Protocol (VOIP) – even the answering machine is new. My life has been about in-your-face technology from start to present.[5] Not for us the 'foolproof mobiles' like Japan's ultra low-tech S-Phone, made for technophobe Baby Boomers.[6]

The role of technology in national success is increasing and we are the people who know and exploit that technology best. As Simon Moss, a 22-year-old Melburnian, told me:

> The role of technology in our lives is absolutely massive – it affects how we relate to people, how we solve problems, how we find information, how we use information. A lot of the new really ground-breaking

ideas that will emerge in the next 15 years will have so much to do with new ways of communicating ... Five years ago the internet was not very useful ... now it makes people a lot more accountable and this generation is really going to capitalize on that phenomenon. We can't live in our own little isolated suburban backyards ... it's just not going to work; people are going to want to get involved and know virtually anything we want – and that's a massive difference.

Young people have led the take-up of all these technologies. Indeed, young women are leading the technology revolution. If you want to see the product of second-wave feminism and the vanguard of women's achievements in the 21st century look at their high-tech trend setting. On another level writer and promoter Tim Duggan described to me how our relationship with technology actually gives us a different mindset to older people. 'We have redefined the idea of accountability,' Tim says. 'It is virtually impossible to have extended periods of time to yourself. It becomes a matter of extreme urgency if someone cannot be tracked down, within five minutes anywhere in the world.'

These shifts are important, but we rarely see an overall analysis of what they mean at a mass level unless it's economically quantifiable. It's no longer news that e-commerce is helping people shop quicker; everyone knows that. Almost everyone has a mobile phone. They know DVD has killed the VCR, that digital cameras are wiping film cameras and film itself from our stores. The question I want to consider is: How does all this make people under 30 different from their parents and grandparents? Are those differences catalysts for other distinctions between the generations in terms of their beliefs and actions at political and social levels?

Almost all teenagers today are able to achieve a level of independence that wasn't possible for their parents and unheard of for their grandparents. 'Our generation has mobile phones with them 24 hours a day, 7 days a week.'[7] Today it's possible to do the 'being a teenager' thing without anyone else needing to know. You don't have to sneak downstairs to call to arrange for your friend to drive by at midnight for underage clubbing or a joint down the park – you can text them. Many people feel that the security blanket of the group date is unnecessary now that real-time advice is available from remote friends when your date is in the bathroom. Gay and lesbian teenagers don't need to out themselves to their parents or pick up at the local public toilet to ask questions about their sexuality – they can discreetly contact any number of telephone help-lines or support websites.

Yet it's in our command of the Internet that young people really come to the fore. We run web businesses before we're done with Year 10 and teach ourselves the skills and knowledge to navigate the world. Email and the Internet change the way we view our workplaces – we assume things *must* be done fast and we have little comprehension of or patience for tedious bureaucracy. 'Deadlines have become shorter, work has become quicker to accomplish. Getting a quote from a client that took a couple of days during the era of mail and fax is now an instant process.'[8]

The Internet is simply part of daily existence. This is a different and better headspace to the older mass media mindset. Our Internet proficiency delivers more than highly-paid jobs and a new means for self-expression – we actually have a quicker, cheaper, deeper lifestyle than those who don't use the Internet. We use it to fly across the continent half-price and take in theatre on the cheap. It means we don't have to do any of the things our parents might have. We don't need to sleep out for tickets to events or buy newspapers or go door-to-door looking for part-time jobs. The exact locations of our social engagements can be tracked down in minutes. There is no friend or lover who will dump us because, yet again, we couldn't find the right gift. There are no illnesses or diseases for which we cannot research the symptoms. There are all sorts of gates to be crashed in our world and now we have the information to crash through them.

The bottom line? We lead a much grander lifestyle than our incomes suggest, we solve problems in a flash and we've read about the latest dumb thing George Bush said before most of you have even turned up to the office. All this puts our generation at a tremendous competitive advantage and gives us a different set of social and political perspectives.

Digital technologies

The crucial relevance of digital technologies to the trajectory of our generation should not be underestimated.

> We are entering an era where everything is going digital. It's going to be the main event of our lives for decades to come. The digital age is bringing about the democratization of information, the removal of traditional barriers of time, distance and wealth, and the onset of total transparency.[9]

The traditional television business model, to pick an example, is now 'out the window'. Narrowcasting, niche audiences, skipping technology and the anaesthetizing effects of media saturation are far more powerful than the lure of the sleep inducing free-to-air TV we put up with now. With a decent policy framework it is certain digital TV would boom in Australia, as it has elsewhere and as other digital technologies have.

From the first generation of peer-to-peer networking software like Napster through to the latest likes of Bit Torrent – 500 times more powerful that Napster and now responsible for one-third of all traffic on the Internet (it allows entire high quality movies and TV programs to be downloaded and shared easily) – the trend is for communities of interest to demand ways to enjoy that interest using the latest digital technology.[10] Again and again old institutions, from music studios to the US Department of Homeland Security and the

PLEASE JUST F* OFF . . . IT'S OUR TURN NOW

Motion Picture Association of America, have attempted to prosecute these communities into submission. It didn't work with music – look at the iPod phenomena which developed as a useful money making exercise within the download paradigm – and it won't work with movies either.

The texting juggernaut

If you asked a telecommunications executive in the 1990s whether they thought short messages on mobile phones would revolutionise social structures within and between generations, they would have said no. As it happened young people appropriated SMS, or texting, for their own social purposes. When we gained the ability to send messages between phone networks in April 2000 a 600 percent increase in text messages was achieved in six months and the exponential rise in popularity has continued.[11] Now many prefer texting to making a call and the practice is so out of control that German psychotherapist Andreas Herter seriously proposes that *'text message addiction is a real and serious illness because it causes mental and financial damage.'* Indeed, we sent more than two billion text messages in Australia in 2004 and the phone carriers describe their customers as 'mainly young', while the first person to use the loss of their thumb because of over-texting was a 14-year-old.

More positively, as the first generation to embrace texting, we are also the first to experience the new identities and communities that texting enables. You might even be tempted to call us 'Generation Text', if you were in marketing.[12] As a Finnish student, Eija-Liisa Kasaniemi, wrote in her dissertation:

> Through SMS teens hate, gossip, mediate, and express longing, even when the writer lacks the courage for a call or in situations where the other communication channels are inappropriate ... The SMS phenomenon has generated its own terminology, customs and social

norms ... perhaps the most surprising feature in the text messaging of Finnish teenagers is the extent to which it incorporates collective behaviour. Text messages are circulated among friends, composed together, read together.[13]

It has even been revealed by a Motorola survey that Australian teenagers would prefer to receive a fun SMS to a Christmas card. My favourite SMS moment came in October 2003. A friend from high school texted me from her couch in Sydney as she was watching *Captain Corelli's Mandolin* to ask me about one of the finer points of fascism. At the time I was walking around a park in Madrid on a tour of the Spanish Civil War frontline. Turning to ask our guide, I was able to text her with what she needed within two minutes and for 40 cents!

Virtual communities

Mobile phones and the Internet mean information that was out of reach is now at our fingertips. The sheer critical mass and the multiplicity of ideas and messages that exist in virtual communities are their attraction. You only have to give a little of yourself – whether it be time, personal information or ideas – to be a part of these communities, but you get much more back. The cost of retrieving information or solving a problem is negligible and these communities allow more people to cooperate more often than ever before.

All the successful e-commerce enterprises are based on this cooperation and lending of reputation to facilitate a higher community good. Think of eBay and Amazon – neither would work without the recommendation systems that encourage people to trust. eBay proudly advertises that 99.99 percent of auctions are successfully completed. eBay founder Pierre Omidyar built eBay as a 'place where people can come together' and it is trust and reputation that has allowed these markets and communities to grow.[14]

Trust is integral to a successful virtual community and it is a core ingredient of social capital. Through the example of trust we see that the mainstreaming of computer technologies has promoted far stronger communities than commentators such as Robert Putnam and Lindsay Tanner in their books *Bowling Alone* and *Crowded Lives* admit.

Virtual communities do come with difficulties, however. 'Today there's more written communication, more mediated communication which isn't a positive thing necessarily. It's less physical and less affectionate,' explains Gwen Carpenter. Her friend, Christian Ahlert, an expert from the Oxford Internet Institute, agreed as we discussed the pros and cons of our information overloaded lives. 'I feel quite detached from local life sometimes. I have travelled a lot and I find people I belong to are not in any single given place and that is sometimes difficult.' But then, 'Without the Internet I couldn't have met a lot of my friends – that's a cool thing.'

Two way changes

Whether it's GPS (Global Positioning Systems), Blackberries or Personal Diary Assistants (PDAs) – technology doesn't muck around at the edges. It not only lets us do new things, it changes the way we do everything. In accumulative fashion it ends up changing our very being. Gene Becker of Hewlett Packard says it is only a matter of years before 'every person, place or thing can be connected wirelessly, anywhere in the world, through the Web.'[15] And while technology lets us *be* new things we also seize technology and craft new purposes for it that were never intended – as we have seen in the overview of texting.

If you want to see the ultimate representation of how our generation expresses itself to the rest of the world then focus your attention on 'video mash-ups'. This is the art of stealing images and sound from many iconic movies or video clips and mashing them into the one quick and dirty piece of audio-visual entertainment. You see them as backdrops in clubs, as the graphics in homemade desktop publications, in cult attachments emailed to offices across the world. Video mash-ups are a vibrant and utterly original medium, yet they're shamelessly derived from other people's creative work. None of the material or the mediums was created with the intended uses of being part of a video-mash up, yet we make it happen. Very us.

Blogging

Blogs are important because they represent the opposite of concentrated media ownership. Generations before us might have been satisfied with the letters pages of newspapers as a voice in important debates – we are not, as I discuss in more detail in Chapter 10, 'The Australian Mediocracy'. Blogs can be anything from a teenage girl's personal diary to a rabid dissection of some New World Order. Blogs are unfiltered grassroots opinion and they get credibility because other people link to them, not because Rupert Murdoch approves of them.

Regardless of your appetite for blogs they are balancing the power between audiences and the media elite. They're also creating conversations between journalists and audiences that simply didn't exist when the passive audience had only the letters page as a voice.[16] Ninety percent of blogs are created by people under 30. It's popular because it's easy and our educated population likes the idea of having its own voice. We want conversations not lectures in this age.

Collective action and technology

Whether it's texting, eBay, chat rooms, blogging or peer-to-peer networking – there is a common thread: collective action. This fact sits next to the reluctance of older activists to embrace the opportunities new technologies offer. This is a serious flaw in their attitude to social change. The Internet 'creates a global public space' and is an essential tool in any political campaign.[17] Christian Ahlert has studied use of the Internet for nearly a decade and was clear when telling me about older Internet users, 'they use the Internet how they would use other media, but they don't see how you can do things differently. They are very afraid of it'.

People over 35 will, when coaxed, set up an email list they can post from – but usually not one that allows a full discussion. This rather redundant act is then celebrated as an achievement. If they join an Internet group discussion list they often can't figure out how to post and stay a silent member. Or my favourite trick – setting up just one email address for a whole organisation or a one-page website that is rarely updated and then complaining that the Internet and email aren't delivering all the benefits young people promise. Many senior politicians still can't or won't check their email inbox – yet young people are allegedly the activists who don't measure up!

If you want to know how the youth-heavy 'anti-globalisation' movement was able to get organised so quickly you can save the hassle of reading *No Logo* and remember one word – Yahoogroups. Yahoogroups are free email discussion lists on every conceivable topic that have a message archive, allow you to upload files and communicate with hundreds of like-minded people simply by addressing your email to the name of the group. I'm a member of 65 of these groups. Joining a selection of Yahoogroups designed for Baby Boomers was instructive – they just don't get the concept. In February 2004 I joined groups like '**lateboomers@yahoogroups.com**' (for people born between 1958 and 1963), '**highIQboomers@yahoogroups.com**' and '**anti-aging@yahoogroups.com**'. The members – and there were hundreds – are to be applauded for trying, unlike most of their peers. However, when they complain that young people don't know who Carole King is and, rather than organizing something, waste time writing things like 'why do they scrutinize (us) so much . . . we are not selfish, I agree. It was our generation who did so much . . . I am sooooo tired of being examined and commented upon. No other generation has ever faced this kind of scrutiny,' it can be frustrating.[18]

While protesting and dropping-out are the main models by which Boomers understand dissent, young people today have a much more sophisticated understanding of the concept. Culture jamming is mainstream amongst young activists yet it exists in a separate orbit, separate to those people who think a petition is an effective way to be heard (note: MPs throw petitions in the bin). This re-appropriation of brands; whether 'McShit' T-Shirts, computer hackers redesigning official websites or slogans like 'Baby Gap – old enough to wear them, old enough to make them' sure beats 'hey hey, ho ho, Bad person X has got to go'.

Clever, but limited. That sums up the critique provided by culture jamming, an admission that critics of capitalism do not have a genuine alternative. The critique is not offered by people interested in violence or revolution, but by people who are sick of reality not resembling rhetoric – of being sold a dream that can easily become a nightmare. Further down the chain of interest is the apolitical version of culture jamming – the more widespread habit of cultural referencing.

In the other direction there are new protest forms that go beyond culture jamming. At the NSW Branch of the National Union of Students a hardy team of activists in 2000 and 2001 became pioneers in organizing effective protest actions via SMS. What we did was organise small scale 'snap actions' – called at an hour's notice. We would take over an intersection, perhaps, parading signs to motorists reading 'Youth wages are slave wages', or descend upon John Howard's electorate office, barging in and taking camera crews with us into his inner sanctum, doing interviews from behind his desk. Small stuff, sure. But exciting, highly effective and not possible without new technology and a willingness to experiment with new ways of communicating.

If the *Guardian* newspaper is to be believed, the protests we toyed with as the millennium dawned were chiefly responsible for the downfall of the right-wing Spanish government in that country's March 2004 elections.

> The message stretched far beyond Madrid. By that evening, PP (conservative party) branches all over Spain were being harangued on the night before the general election by demonstrators not allied to any political party... Most remarkable of all, the protests were organized in just a few hours, via text message and email, by a disillusioned electorate that had decided to take matters into its own hands.[19]

Yet for all the dramatic possibilities of new technology, nothing can replace face-to-face communication which takes up more of our time and energy than any other type of communication.

Yoof and language

The rumour that young people's slang is causing the death of the Queen's English is not grounded in any common sense. I'm not ashamed to write in bullet point form if it gets the message across. Life isn't a novel. I don't give a toss about Lynne Truss and her cohort of punctuation Nazis or her monologue on manners. When I think of all the world's pressing ills, the incorrect use of apostrophes doesn't really rate.

Besides, young people misuse English as a defence mechanism as much as we do it out of ignorance. I say 'like', 'seriously', and 'literally' as a protection against the lies that are pumped into me from every angle, every day. We are so unused to truth and transparency and so surrounded by fantasy that we qualify our statements by re-emphasising that our statements are not like those falsehoods. He was 'literally' about to walk in front of a car, because we've all seen a hundred movies where people look like they die, but it's all a trick.

Our humour might be silly, but that is irrelevant to a discussion about our ability to communicate with language. I find it funny to read sentences like those sent to me in a 'forward' email one day in late 2004:

- 'Her vocabulary was as bad, as, like, whatever.'
- 'The revelation that his marriage of 30 years had disintegrated because of his wife's infidelity came as a rude shock, like a surcharge at a formerly surcharge-free ATM.'
- 'It hurt the way your tongue hurts after you accidentally staple it to the wall.'

It is language like this that forms the basis of the thousands of conversational codes that permeate our friendship networks – they mean much to us and little to anyone else, much like our approach to cultural referencing.

Cultural referencing

Given the lack of cultural icons our generation has been allowed to develop (in a media we don't control) we are forced to find cultural bonds in the oddest and saddest ways. We even turn to our childhoods for communication inspiration. I especially enjoy competitions at house parties to remember story lines from childhood TV shows – from *Astroboy* to *The Mysterious Cities of Gold* and *Degrassi*. Forget *Starsky and Hutch* and *Batman Who Won't F*cking Go Away* – when are they going to do a remake of all those shows from my childhood? One step removed from all that are retro-chic trends like the cult of *Hello Kitty* and the *Transformers* revival.

In all this, there is more than meets the eye. In addition to people running around wearing altered Nike shirts with 'just stop it' under the tick, thousands of personal conversational codes permeate friendship networks across the country. Based on reusing or reshaping lines from classic videos, *Kath and Kim, Little Britain* or email networks like *popbitch* we create little parallel universes for ourselves. These shows and websites don't have one literal meaning and their impact cannot be measured using old notions such as quality or popularity – these are not the yardsticks social groups of my generation apply.

This cultural referencing is now beginning to infiltrate the mainstream media. Across the English-speaking world headlines and puns now incorporate iconic shows like *The Office*, *Sex and the City* and *Friends*. From sex discrimination suits to street prostitution, no topic can escape a reference. Yet the majority of Australians have never watched any of these shows, and none except *Friends* will ever top the ratings.

The main point about these shows is that their impact is deep rather than broad. They connect most with the rich, smart and up-and-coming under-35s. These people lead fashions and will, eventually, lead public debates – so it follows that what they watch matters. What they watch are withering shows (*Simpsons*, *The Office*), clever shows (*Friends*, *West Wing*, *Will and Grace*), and cool shows specific to their lives (*Sex and the City*, *Secret Life of Us*).

You will also notice that these shows are not a) soaps, b) infotainment, or c) variety. That's because the people that will shape this country over the next 20 years have a little more self-respect than to spend Saturday night watching Daryl Somers and Denise Drysdale or *The Bill*. Failing to understand this basic point might leave you room to understand surburbia but you will not understand the future of power in Australia.

I would love to have a 9 to 5 job, but for anyone who wants to succeed I just don't think that exists. If you put in the hours you reap the rewards. If you work hard while you're young you can travel and retire early. I'm happy to work long hours if I enjoy my job – you don't notice the hours when you love what you're doing.

Paula, 22, Darwin

FOR all their self-proclaimed radicalism the Boomers were married with a mortgage, children and a career by 25.

Bernard Salt

CHAPTER FOUR

Secret lives of us

Groups and networks

If you want to understand young people today you ought to understand the difference between networks and clubs. Clubs are groups – they are formal and removed from our daily activities. Groups are full of strong ties and consist of few people. They are the sun around which the networks orbit – important for stability but stifling if you get too close. Networks and their weak ties fill the social galaxy. Groups have dominated the lives and the social and economic activities of Boomers in a way that networks influence the lives of my peers.

Our world is not framed by nations, natural resources and industry in the way it was just two generations ago. We are now globally networked and more information-driven.[1] The world we live in is too complex and chaotic to be controlled in the way individuals or companies or nations have exercised control in the 20th century. Yet most of the organisations and institutions that figure prominently in Australian life have grown vertically under a system of 'command and control'. In the future it is all about horizontal connections. What's important is being able to adapt and take opportunities when they arise. You are playing the wrong game if you think power and influence and even fun is about being in control anymore.

Hierarchies can't cope with the new complex world we live in unless they are rigidly enforced, as is the case with armed forces. Effective hierarchies are needed for disaster situations like Hurricane Katrina on the US Gulf Coast and their absence in that case hurt thousands, but they aren't needed for most things in our lives. Ordinary people don't accept such rigidity any more and it therefore becomes inevitable that effective models of communication and decision-making have few or no hierarchical principles.

Networks are designed to negate hierarchy – their members collaborate rather than compete. Networks are inherently flexible and they are more capable of sharing learning amongst their members than hierarchies.[2] They are ideally suited to an era of rapid change. They are increasingly democratic and diverse and because of these features they will be the lasting legacies of our generation.

Barry Wellman, the Canadian founder of the International Network for Social Network Analysis, has created the term that is the typical outlook of my generation: 'networked individualism'. This means we understand we live in a wider world but we are individuals first. We build social lives around the identities we choose for ourselves, rather than allow our identities to be dictated by our geographic or class communities.

All this can be very threatening to older people who have grown up with particular types of community and only understand how to deal with particular types of hierarchy and bureaucracy. An anecdote conveyed to me by Cameron Neil of the International Young Professionals Foundation demonstrates this:

> The networks I am involved in are about forming new bonds of trust and co-operation. It's based on wanting to make the world a better place but as the same time develop new skills and master new challenges. The night before a speech I gave to a Rotary conference I was talking

with people (Rotarians) . . . I look at Rotary and it freaks me out – it's just so structured. Belonging to a club where you go to breakfast every week, where you turn up and do the same thing over and over again, it has no appeal to me.

Placeless community

As we saw in the overview of virtual communities, individuals can now undertake previously communal activities on their own. Communities can exist without any physical anchor, and they can come together in any number of changing locations. This transforms the whole notion of collectivity that we have developed since the Industrial Revolution.

While it is not much studied, I would argue information technology is much better at sustaining existing communities than creating new ones. When I moved to the UK in 2003, I didn't find the Internet very useful for finding new friends or romantic dates, but I did find it incredibly useful as a budget means of keeping old friendships alive and tracking down existing contacts in London. The Southern Cross Group – the body for Australian Expatriates – is also well aware of how IT can sustain diaspora communities. They are experiencing phenomenal interest and are now in touch with tens of thousands of Australians in any given week, via email. Given the massive distances between people and places in Australia, the intensity of its diaspora across the world and our historical role as an early adopter of technology, Australians, and more particularly young Australians, are prime candidates to be remembered as pioneers of placeless community.

Social networks of friends – are they the new family?

It's wrong to think you can understand our social networks with simple ideas of role-swapping, like friends replacing family. That said, our friendship networks are a vital source of cultural capital. It's the 21st century version of 'who you know' – 'pulling strings' is not a tool of the upper middle class or intellectual elite any more, it's a pro-active tool almost anyone can use to lift themselves up career and social ladders. That has to be good.

Even so, the concept of 'Urban Tribes', popularised by the American author Ethan Watters is an insight into the real life *Secret Life of Us* and these groups will define our times. As Chris Chesher has written in the *Griffith Review*, 'we live in a network society and share a network culture', and the most important networks are social.[3] They are delivering social change to their core members and generating political change as a by-product.

These stories aren't considered real stories by Baby Boomers – they are seen as evidence of an extended adolescence. That attitude ignores a fundamentally radical truth – we are the first generation whose relationships are driven by choice rather than obligation. Not merely amongst close friends, or our partners and lovers – but all our relationships. Our stories are stories of the widest networks of any generation and the special ways that we manage and use these 'weak ties' for individual and collective advantage. These networks don't fill academic journals but they are solid evidence that Robert Putnam's findings in *Bowling Alone* (that young people just don't have a civic spirit and are screwing society by not joining groups) are junk science.

Friendships for today's youth take place on a whole new level from other generations. This social glue was provided in the past by marriages and choking family bonds. So, while our mass movement of friendships might look flimsy, they withstand a lot more pressure than their predecessor social units. They don't wither in our twenties,

PLEASE JUST F* OFF . . . IT'S OUR TURN NOW

nor are they as dependent on geographic proximity. They deliver stability in an uncertain world, are sources of truth in seas of lies and hard sells, and become networks of complete solidarity helping us to achieve happiness. They do this better than a destiny laid out for you by family or class ever could. As Aristotle said: 'without friends no one would choose to live.'

Mass consequences follow from this. These networks are replacing traditional and explicitly public civic organizations with a more honest and meaningful way for people to develop themselves and each other. These networks might not build as many barbecue shelters as Lions clubs do and they don't raise funds for school equipment, but that's because they are not concerned with constructing facades to hide a deeper social malaise. Today's friendship networks are about improving individual self-esteem and working together to make each other better, happier people. You can bet these friendship networks have rescued a lot of people out of abusive relationships, saved countless more from self-harm or addictions, and provide the support that families should, but often don't, offer. My own core friendship network is dominated by people who have moved to Sydney from the country or other far-flung places; people who are different for a whole range of reasons. Between the many layers of this network we have provided each other with a level of support and comfort that no external service or our absent families could ever provide. We were thrown together because we were all searching for things that traditional social structures – home towns, nuclear families, houses of religion, even Prozac – had not been able to provide. We've built an understanding that complements and extends the understanding our families have of us, even though they have known us for much longer. In cases where it hasn't been possible or desirable to maintain those family relationships our network has become the family. I know thousands of others who feel they get and give the same things in their own networks and that makes me proud of the things my generation can achieve.

Our friendships networks are the greatest social movement we have. They don't announce themselves with banners and chants ('whadda we want – sex and chocolate and touch footy and shopping – when do we want it – now!') but they are living showcases of our progressive values and our humanity. The things that make our networks great aren't celebrated in popular culture – but we know they exist and we need to remind ourselves of them more often.

> BOOMERS find it difficult to understand how we can have so many close relationships with people that are not romantic . . . I can talk about things with my friends that my parents could never talk about with theirs.
>
> *Scott Carn, 26, Sydney*

We accept people into these networks regardless of their sexuality, we mix in ethnically diverse circles, and we do not have gender barriers when it comes to leadership roles and getting the necessary things done to sustain the friendships. While we can't implement all this in our workplaces or governments, we're doing our level best to live out our beliefs in places where we know we can make a difference. In our friendship networks you aren't a failure for not delivering kids and a mortgage. You don't have to have a particular profession, or great hand-eye coordination to qualify for membership. You can even move to another continent. You get to be one of the team because of who you are and you get to stay on the team for years and years and years. All this is more liberating in a personal sense than anti-discrimination legislation, a dole cheque or most of the outcomes of the social movements of generations before us.

Scouting groups and knitting circles and church aren't the answers to the problems we face today. I have absolutely no desire to form a meaningful relationship with people just because they live in my street; I make friends with people because I like them not because ancient homespun 'wisdom' says I should.

Our social movements are about allowing people to exercise the freedoms that have long existed on paper but rarely in practice. Don't beg governments to give it to you – because in many instances you can just be it. This is an achievement fought for and won by young people today – and it can't be wound back. That's real social change.

Relationships, sexuality and self-esteem

No one needs another book about this, but bear with me for a page. The consensus is: 'there's no rule book for relationships these days.' Every month there's a new box or label for our primal urges. We hear about 'Contrasexuals' (women like Samantha from *Sex and the City*), 'Smug Marrieds' and 'Singletons' (from *Bridget Jones' Diary*) and 'Metrosexuals' (blokes who moisturise and dress properly). When asked by Sydney's *Sun-Herald*, representatives of the Manly Youth Council struggled to define a healthy sexual relationship. 'Eventually they came up with three principles: respect, communication and "being able to be an individual".'[4] The point is we don't have a special category for romantic relationships anymore. We often use the same rules to manage them as we do our friends. There is a blurring between the boundaries of our monogamous relationships, our casual flings and our friendship circles. It's not unusual for whole groups of friends to have slept with each other at different points in time – which one comes first, the friendships or the sex, is very much 'chicken and egg' these days.

Another salient issue is the difficulty people have in loving others if they haven't learnt to love themselves. Says one 27-year-old from Sydney:

> A lot of us have had dysfunctional upbringing. We understand that you have to be happy with who you are to actually make a difference and to be a good person and to have a successful relationships. Everyone I talk to who has a similar upbringing is saying they understand their responsibilities 'but I have to be OK with who I am', first.

Germaine Greer famously reversed her commitment never to write a sequel to *The Female Eunuch* on the basis that in 1970s girls weren't cutting their wrists and throwing up their lunches in toilets in any great number. Boys fare no better. You are now more likely to commit suicide when you are young than when you are old. Depression isn't just a profitable industry, it's a reflection of a collective trauma that exists in my generation. How else to you explain the average American child experiencing more anxiety than psychiatric patients their age in the 1950s?[5]

It comes as no surprise to me that *New Scientist* recently found that there are as many genuinely asexual people in the world today as there are homosexual. Not being interested in sex is a legitimate choice in the eyes of my peers, just as being anywhere on the gay scale of 1–10 is utterly fine. But staying a virgin until you are married? Bonkers say 90 percent of us. As one of my interview subjects insisted: 'sexuality is an issue where we have built on the earlier work of the boomers and really pushed it further.'

But in between wrist-slitting, anorexia, low self-esteem, being 'the only gay in the village', AIDS, safe sex, asexuality and Samantha from *Sex and the City*, the majority of people are still able and willing to begin a family. And when they do, according to research by Barbara Pocock and Jane Clarke for The Australia Institute, 'many' young people plan to run different families and be different types of parents then their own parents were. Specifically, the boys want to be more active fathers and the girls want to more equally share the tasks of earning and caring within their families.

Career kangaroos

'We started out', says Hilary McPhee, who in 1975 co-founded the 'legendary' independent Australian publishers McPhee Gribble, 'with an ethos rather than a profit-motive, an idea rather than a money-making venture ... for most of our 15 years we had the luxury of a

> workplace where other priorities ruled... All of us wore old clothes and drove small secondhand cars covered in dents... We earned around a school-teacher's wage most of the time. Everything else was re-invested in employing the people we needed in order to publish the books we wanted. It was a way of working as remote now as the moon.'[6]

It was a classic progressive Baby Boomer venture. And now it's like a fairytale from another age. It can amuse us, we might even dream about it, but we can't own it anymore than we can be Cinderella. Work is different today.

> WHEN I was in my teens and early twenties I thought life would progress in a linear fashion ... School. Uni. Travel. Job. Kids. Mortgage ... But that just doesn't happen. Work places enormous demands on your time you just can't walk out at 5 o'clock, but you can walk out of a dinner party to pick up work ... if you don't have the commitment you are really frowned upon in your career.
>
> *Brigid, 27, Sydney*

Brigid has touched on the tip of an iceberg with that assessment. But the extra demands of the 21st-century workplace are situated on a two-way street. If we can't get what we want from an employer, we'll just move on.

> ... the average person now goes through eight jobs before the age of 32 ... as a generation that has grown up around technology, we have low attention spans and we're always looking for the next best thing.[7]

Personally, I've had a dozen jobs in eight years. I'm happy with that, it's still two fewer than the number of houses I've lived in during the same time. Most of us adjusted to the concept that there is no such thing as a job for life in about, oh, 1987. There are important consequences to this understanding though.

> A lot people are saying: 'I'm not going to work in something that I hate' I am not going to retire at 65 having spent 40 years doing something I hate. We're not dumb, we're not passive recipients of this. If we're not going to have job security anyway we may as well do something we enjoy and have it now.
>
> Cameron Neil, 29, Canberra.
International Young Professionals Foundation

Having responded quickly to this reality we now face the complaint that loyalty is only CV-deep. Not true. We are simply perceptive and nimble, able to spot opportunities and use them. We love work and we love to be challenged. The fact is, ambitious staff are less loyal and they always have been.[8] What is different now is that my generation is full of ambitious people compared to more docile generations of previous eras. The fact that I wouldn't be prepared to work for the minimum wage has nothing to do with being a 'job snob' or a 'dole bludger,' as I found when interviewing my peers:

> I don't get out of bed for less than $25 an hour, but I don't mind doing unpaid work. One company pays me $80 an hour. I do 20 hours a week paid work and 25 hours a week volunteer work. That's the advantage of being creative and entrepreneurial and I can give back.
>
> Simon Moss, 22

We demand a lot from work and have the capacity to obtain it. Let's call us 'career kangaroos'.

Recruitment company Talent2 found in 2004 that 74 percent of employees are changing jobs more frequently than ever before. The reasons? They aren't getting career opportunities and employees weren't willing be give loyalty to corporations. A third of us are now scanning the job sections and registering with headhunting companies on the first day in our new jobs.[9] And why not? When your employer has as much loyalty as a Super League player, what's the point in tying yourself down. More than a third of staff think they'll be working for someone else in 12 months time and up to half of all graduate recruits leave within two years.[10] They have reasons to be confident.

> The Dotcom bubble trained up a whole generation of young entrepreneurs. They rode it up, they rode it down – they came out. They're still 32 or 33 years old ... The greatest entrepreneurial generation of the last 50 years.

So says Paul Saffo, Director of the Institute of the Future, based in the US.

What do we want from employers?

Today's career kangaroos are a hop ahead. We are fans of 'gold dusting' – the practice of picking jobs and employers that look good on a CV for the purpose of attracting future employers. The point? No matter how lean and mean your corporate machine it can never be more agile than a confident individual with two degrees and an attitude to match.

So what are our demands? Let's start with serious career development opportunities. Quick promotion, company-sponsored post-graduate education, and management who understand ethics are not just for mission statements. *Nine to five* is a DVD with Dolly Parton and Jane Fonda – not a workplace policy.

We are known to support new forms of workplace collectivism like internal democratic processes and team meetings and time sovereignty. Professional associations and the networks they build are attractive, but trade union membership is seen more as a form of insurance than a badge of honour.

So what factors will delay or speed up the inevitable switching of roles and employers? A look at the major trends in human resources over the past decade gives us a clue – employees are rejecting old style offices and old style corporate hierarchies. If we want to work from home – then we will; if we want flexi-time and 10 a.m.–6 p.m. hours – then you better give it to us; if we want open and regular dialogue and team meetings – just try saying no. If you can construct a business case that shows that your choice to work flexibly will have neutral or positive effects for your employer then the law and trade unions should protect that choice for you.

Allowing hopeless managers to remain hopeless is another big turn-off.

> Some awful stuff gets written about Generation X, such as advice from USA Today on 'how to motivate Generation X' that includes 'help them carve up the job into bite-size chunks so they can see the day-to-day results' and move from 'six-month or 12-month reviews to frequent, accurate, specific and timely feedback.' Short of advising that Xers be tucked up into their favourite blanket for an afternoon nap after a glass of milk, it is difficult to see how this advice could be more patronising.[11]

Sometimes you feel as though your generation's insistence on quality is held up as incompetence. I have now lost count of the times line managers and senior staff issue vague instructions where only they know what they mean but refuse to revisit the issue. Then there is the popular breed who insist things be done their way and their way only, often because they can't be bothered to imagine that it can be done differently. I have no patience with an audible sigh when I want feedback on my work or need to discuss how a project is going. Around the country I got the same story:

> I quit the bakery because I had a really rude manager. She had no idea about what she was doing; she got the job because she was an older person. She wouldn't let me ask

questions – she would just tell me: 'mop the floor'. As soon as I don't enjoy the working environment, I quit. I work far better if I respect who I'm working under. If I don't respect them I do a crappy job, I couldn't care what they thought because I don't respect them. I have no passion. If I have faith I'll put in 100 percent. If I think the boss is a moron, I just don't want to be there.

Paula, 22, Darwin

What do we bring to the party?

You'd be right to think it unbalanced to slag off a whole generation as bad managers without at least explaining why young people are generally better at the task. When given the opportunity to be managers in our workplaces we often take different approaches. Our ethics and experience of working in teams and networks rather than hierarchies makes us skilled at consulting when devising strategies and work plans. Good managers ask for feedback on how they are performing their role. Good managers are happy when their staff achieve their development goals and move on. Good managers share the credit for success. And the really good ones take their staff out for team meetings and lunches. We also have enough self-confidence and resilience to want to work with our subordinates rather than simply use them. If we can construct small teams – of three or four or five – we will, because three heads are better than one and no one wants a committee.

This adaptability does not only refer to specific roles in an organisation, but also to our capacity to work for all sorts and sizes of organisations. A real benefit of the constant cycles of change we live in, and tangible evidence that we are a global generation, is our ability to do things to scale. Scalability is the capacity to retain or impart a skill or attribute or undertake a task no matter the situation.

We could be giving a work presentation to our team or doing it via video conference to the company's global headquarters. We can take what we read on a US online news magazine and make it relevant to our company intranet. We can take a local fight against a sweatshop and turn it into an international boycott campaign within a week. This skill is not unique to my generation, but for us it is the norm rather than the exception. And it is worth a bomb to the people who can make use of it.

So we've now established that my generation are great in the workplace, great at relationships and honest about community . . . so what's the catch?

CHAPTER FIVE

So we screwed up

OK. So I've slagged off the Boomers for being the most over-hyped product since Demtel's Bedazzler. And having self-scored my generation as 11 out of 10, it would be a pity to be written off as the secret twin of those dodgy Russian figure-skating judges. That means it's time now for the bad news. You Boomers are getting one slot for revenge, and there's no encore.

It's true – ours is a conflicted generation. We are exposed to so much and want so much that it's hard to make sense of it all. The result: we're often not very coherent. Of course you can make good sense on individual points without any need for coherency across the board – but it does help. What's more, we've never faced massive and absolute adversity on a collective scale. We are poorer for it.

When you have so much time to analyse and relatively little to worry about it's also tempting to exaggerate or write off every difficulty as the fault of others. But that perspective is about thinking the world's problems will be solved without you having to change any of your own actions. It demonstrates a lack of self-confidence and honesty about our role as agents of change. If we're to be a generation worth remembering, we have to take responsibility for fixing our own problems and the problems of Australia at large. If we can't do that we are just a different but equally bad version of the Boomers.

There is no quarterlife crisis

Boomers have given themselves a bad name with their rose-tinted nostalgia industry, so it's unwise for my generation to emulate their self-absorption with a crisis industry of our own. Perhaps our over-zealous self-analysis is a symptom of being surrounded by self-help books our entire lives, I'm not sure. Whatever the case, not one person reading this book is the victim of famine. It's also very likely that you've escaped a clitorectomy or avoided being one of the world's 211-million child slaves.[1] Or, as 24-year-old Sunita Patradoon put it to me: 'It's hard to feel sorry for a group of people whose biggest problem is their iPod broke down.'

The quaterlife crisis is a myth. The only person who can create a quarterlife crisis is you. You can, of course, face other crises in your mid-twenties but they have nothing to do with you being in your mid-twenties. Citing his belief in this alleged quarterlife crisis plague, one over-worked and highly-paid friend moaned that 'not a single one' of his friends 'knew what they wanted to do with their lives'. My advice was to leave the office before 9 p.m., and see how it changed their perspective.

We have the attention span of fruit-flies

We have been trained to speak in sound bites and now we are beginning to think in them too. It's the 'in one ear, out the other' adage slapped on to a generation. We have a concentration based on short-term memory and spend several years of our lives operating Google and Powerpoint. We forget that life existed before pie charts and we fall into intellectual lives based on 'cut and paste' when there are deeper things to ponder. At length. Without distraction. That we need to remember 20 years later.

The lost art of planning

The pre-arranged meeting or date is dead. It is no longer possible to organise a social meeting with a person under 30 on a Monday for Wednesday and expect them to simply turn up. Pointless phone calls, inane text messages all culminating in being stood up by people who are:

- too disorganised to have a diary
- too able to be late because they can excuse themselves by sms
- too lacking in basic manners to use their technology for good rather than laziness.

We're losing the ability to communicate face-to-face

Perhaps we should be grateful others even turn up to our social events. They are obviously the ones who bothered to show the respect of face-to-face contact. It's all too easy in our world of Internet hooking up, text message happy hour and weekend free calls to stop seeing our loved ones. All our communications options are temptations to lose our physicality and affection. But there is simply no replacement for face-to-face interaction. New technologies should add value not replace the real thing.

Common sense gone AWOL

We are often so busy being Yeppies (Young Experimenting Perfection seekers) unable to commit to love or a career because we can never meet our unreasonable expectations, that we lose touch with the most basic of skills.[2] I couldn't figure out how to put salt in my dishwasher for love or money. The only knot I know is the shoelace one. We've been told we are entitled to personal happiness 24/7 – but what's the point in knowing or believing that if you can't even cook yourself dinner.

We are afraid to offend people

As someone who finds it easier to criticise in private that to someone's face, I sympathize with this trait. How about you? There are so many valid lifestyles and defendable ideas these days that a heated discussion in any diverse group of people is a minefield. Individuality is so central to our identity now that it can be a mortal offence in many social circles to have a strong opinion. We can try to shake off PC, but it's like a tattoo on our brains.

> I think there is this tendency to be tolerant of everything to the point where you don't have an opinion on anything. It's infiltrated us to the extent that we can't really yell at people when they disagree with us. There is no objective right or wrong, just individual choices . . . It's one of the great flaws of our generation.
>
> *Rachel Hills, 23*

We are addicted to cheap air travel

Travel is tempting, and a central part of who we are, yet the environmental destruction caused by the cheap air travel revolution is an unacceptable price to pay. Consider for a moment that aviation is widely recognised as the fastest growing source of greenhouse gas emissions and that emissions at altitude have 2.7 times the environmental impact of those on the ground.[3] Consider also our other obsessions, such as having exactly the right foods at our fingertips all year round. Flying 1 kg of in-season asparagus from California to Australia would use more than 2000 times the energy of a locally-grown equivalent.[4] There's really no way around facts like this and ignoring them will just make us full blown Boomeresque hippy-crits.

Our expectations are too high

It's not that we aren't grateful for Boomer feminist activism, or that most Australians don't have to work in factories any longer. My combined washer/dryer is a helluva lot better than an old copper like my grandma used. It's just that if you spend your whole life being grateful you feel like you are living in *Oliver Twist*. So we do the opposite – take it all for granted and spit in the face of the people who sacrificed for us (our parents) or for society (yes, all those campaigners from the '60s and '70s that we diss). It should be a balance and we don't always strike it. Note to parents re: your sacrifice – I'd be nowhere without you, and I hope I've been worth the agony and money. xx

Engagement with democracy is a two-way street

The expectation that politics has to be more interesting, exciting and relevant can be unrealistic if pushed too far. Whatever the attractions of 'Democracy: Big Brother edition', it is ridiculous to think of government as a soap opera. Parliament isn't there to be sexy and to push all the right buttons. 'If we think politics must look like MTV to merit our attention, then we play a high-risk game, and might end up not liking what we get.'[5]

But Australia's public mediocrity can be quite daunting. On Australia Day 2005 the Governor-General (I forget his name) announced that it was terrible that our youth were losing interest in politics and our pubic institutions. The next story in the news was 'Sniffer dogs bust 120 for drugs'.[6] Party drugs that is – at the Big Day Out (!). Come on, are you saying you can't see the link between the two stories?

But enough self-flagellation. Someone else needs the whips for a porn video.

PART TWO

Slouching towards mediocrity:

Australian under-achievement in focus

A sluggard community which never asks questions or inspects the world around it with a bright eye, and which never tried out different ways of understanding its circumstances, is sure first to stagnate, and then to slip backwards.
Professor A. C. Grayling

THE sad truth is that excellence makes people nervous.
Shana Alexander

When I think of all the things I'd like Australia to be, a 'quiet isolated place with a natural resource-led stable macroeconomic environment' is not one of them. I don't think of Australia's intelligence agencies being 'deficient to the point of being pathetic'.[1] I get seriously scared when *The Economist* tells me our 14 years of economic growth has relied on 'soaring house prices and cheap credit'.[2] Our parliaments are sheltered workshops for social misfits and Bob Jellies. The Cabinet resembles a used car salesman convention. Media players rarely take risks on content, have lost sight of worldwide trends, and operate in a regulatory environment that fell asleep decades ago. They wouldn't recognise digital TV if it slapped them. The corporate sector thinks CSR is a sugar company.

But that's all OK – we're cosmopolitan, remember. We've got Fashion Week and coffee brewed from real beans and someone said Sydney was a world city. As for diversity – well, we all eat Thai now!

But if it's all so fabulous, why do we have a lost generation of more than a million exiles? People usually don't flee world cities, do they? Could it be that most of Sydney and Melbourne resemble

'Springfield' rather than London or New York? Is there really a 'world city' in Australia? Could it be that there's less opportunity than sunshine in this big land of ours and that, even worse, we have 'a public culture sinking under the dead weight of public nostalgia'.[3]

The weather can't explain the entire vapour of mediocrity that clouds Australia's path to progress. But you'll struggle to find a more sophisticated analysis because we don't bother trying to explain our failures and half-efforts. We don't even admit they exist. It's time to get real and say: 'I love Australia, but I don't love mediocrity.'

The longer we pretend these failures don't exist the harder it becomes to recognise new examples. And if we can't recognise mediocrity we won't be able to change it. So that's where we have to start. I suggest a zero-tolerance approach to mediocrity in public life.

This is not a plea that rests on ideological foundations; it is simply about identifying and demanding acceptable standards in public life. What follows is a glance at the problems my generation is jack of and is going to have to fix.

ENOUGH about me. Let's talk about you. What do you think about me?
C.C. Bloom, Beaches

THE real pity is they (Boomers) trashed the place and left us to clean up.
Letter writer to The Age[4]

LIKE a Hollywood star whose beauty is fading, boomers clamour for status . . . the butt of jokes that parody their presumptions to power.
Bernard Salt[5]

NOTHING is more tedious than the front-line recollections of a Sixties radical.
Christopher Hitchens

CHAPTER SIX

Property apartheid and the boomer credibility gap

'Grey power' is coming. The 'new old' is already here – at supermarkets, voting booths and a media outlet near you. The language of 'grey power' is an affirming one. It's all about 'breaking down barriers', 'extending active life', 'society repaying people who've worked hard for decades', and worst of all, 'old people having a voice'. But what oppressed citizenry are we talking about? It is the Iraqis? Down-trodden refugees? The unfairly dismissed? No, it's a group of people who already hog our media space and own most of the country's assets. I don't want to gag and bind pensioners, but these are not your typical near-destitute or invalid OAPs. They do yoga, have big warm homes and can talk under water.

More specifically, I object to the idea that one person's vote is more equal than another. And that's what the concept of the 'grey vote' is all about. It perpetuates the belief that it's more useful to court (translation: pork-barrel) old voters than other groups because there's more of them or they are a greater influence on their communities (insert further bollocks, etc ...). In fact, I'd argue that the 'grey power' set already have too much power and that the whole concept is shonky. If the merits of the 'grey power' movement are debatable now, then the debate will certainly be over when the late Boomers – those born after 1955 – start meeting the definition of 'grey' in about 2015. Currently many pensioners *are* doing it tough, and apart from the cheap bus travel I can see how you'd think it's a bit of a bummer being old. This won't be the case with the late Boomers. Not only will they have had most of their working lives to get their superannuation in order, the government will have given everything else to them for free. If the pension isn't good enough for them, then tough titties.

They shouldn't get special tax breaks; the pension shouldn't increase any more than other welfare payments; and the people of working age who've spent most of their lives paying for most public services should get a bit of respect. Why? Because we're paying for it. Over the next 25 years the growth in Australia's working-age population will gradually slow and eventually come to a halt. Whereas the working age cohort currently increases by 166,000 each year, this rate will decline until about 2026 when it will practically cease to grow at all. The Treasury and leading economic forecasters agree – we have a big inter-generational fiscal problem, and my generation will have to pay.

Moving from matters economic to matters intellectual, social and cultural, the Boomer Credibility Gap starts to yawn open – emphasis on the yawn.

The credibility gap explained

The Soviet Union under Leonid Brezhnev was a joke; new technologies set information free despite the Communists' best efforts at suppression. In the end the official 'line' was so removed from reality that the truth could no longer be hidden. Things were getting better but not *that* much better; life was inefficient and restricted. Still, the Soviet Union carried on in its own universe – destined to unravel in an unexpected but inevitable way. Some couldn't really rise up against

PLEASE JUST F* OFF . . . IT'S OUR TURN NOW

Under-thirties on the over-fifties

For a group of people so obviously reliant on their successor generation's willingness to pay higher taxes in order to fund pensions to keep them in lifestyles to which they have become accustomed, Boomers show an astonishing lack of self-awareness. This is what my peers have to say about this irresponsible generation of mutton dressed up as lamb.

> I just read an article today on 'being rich, fit and frisky' how 'there's never been a better time to be 60'. It made me sick – I want to throw up. Is there nothing these people can't leave alone? They think they invented youth and that they never have to give it up – it's infuriating!
>
> *Jo, 30*

After WWII, they were handed the entire planet on a silver platter. They've pissed the entire thing away. Now younger people must pay while the boomers continue to wallow in their own fucking self-absorption. The boomers invented generational warfare. So, it's time for them to suck it up and take what they've got coming. I didn't appoint myself the arbiter of all things that matter. I'm not the one buying a house in Tuscany while Rome burns. I'm not the one popping a pill every time I feel bad or can't get it up. And I'm not drugging my over-sugared, over-indulged children, either.

Roxanne, age unknown

They take for granted the privileges they had and assume we have the same privileges . . . As if the only thing stopping us achieving what they achieved is ourselves – not the system they created. They don't understand that now, because of the system, they need to do more for the next generation. They're very selfish. They are a generation of users, takers. If they were really interested in world poverty as a generation, then surely something would have changed by now.

Alastair (name changed), 24

PROPERTY APARTHEID AND THE BOOMER CREDIBILITY GAP

> They make out as if they struggled as students and worked really hard to get what they've got. And now it's ALL theirs. They need to acknowledge they got a lot from the system. People from my generation are not given a lot from the system.
>
> *Rachel, 23*

They want to have the exotic around them but they want to be able to turn it on and off like a television instead of it being a part of their lives. They want to go down the street and see a few freaks and second hand clothes stores but they don't want the punks to get drunk at night or for people to make noise.

Anonymous, 28

I'm almost 30 – I'm not young anymore, so why am I made to feel so young?

Gemma, almost 30 (!)

... And a Boomer on his peers:

As convinced of their uniqueness as the Bolsheviks, as persuaded of their genius as the Victorians, as self-absorbed as the Romantics, as prosperous as the ancient Romans, . . . Feared and admired in their youth, today they inspire little more than irritation. The single most damning, and obvious, criticism that can be leveled at Baby Boomers is, of course, that they promised they wouldn't sell out and become fiercely materialistic like their parents, and then they did. They further complicated matters by mulishly spending their entire adult lives trying to persuade themselves and everybody else that they had not in fact sold out, that they had merely matured and grown wiser, that their values had undergone some sort of benign intellectual mutation . . . They're stupefyingly self-centered, unbelievably rude, obnoxious beyond belief, and they're everywhere.

Joe Queenan, author of Balsamic Dreams, A Short but Self-Important History of the Baby Boomer Generation it all, others didn't know how to, and most wouldn't have wanted to bother. Millions lived under a centrally-implemented collective nostalgia. I put it to you that their very own Boomer *nomenklatura* shares many of these characteristics. Like their favourite sitcoms, the Boomers are destined to keep going one season too many.

Much Australian under-achievement can be sourced back to the unwillingness of established power-holders to innovate and allow young Australians to lead that innovation process. If older Australians were less apathetic and more willing to engage with new, energetic but imperfect ideas, then we might be a fairer, richer and better society. To lay it out in black and white: if all those progressive Baby Boomers could surrender some of their grip on institutional and economic power, and try some genuine mentoring of the young, they might get the political change and economic growth they always bleat about. If one-time '60s lefties who love to complain about John Howard shared power with the young they might not have to put up with him any longer. And if all those shamelessly materialistic suburbanite Boomers loosened their grip on the property market they might have even bigger or better plasma TVs. Whatever needs our current systems serve, younger and more energetic people could serve them better. Some of my best friends might be Boomers but sadly for them, in the words of the egalitarian revolutionary Tom Paine, '*he who dares not offend cannot be honest*'.

Look at moiye, young people, look at moiye

The assumption that what you do is of interest to a wide range of others who may or may not know you is peculiar indeed. It's very bourgeois and a key feature of Boomer action. Their brand of activism arose as a form of therapy as often as it did from need. This was very unlike the activist base from earlier generations of trade unionists, religious missionaries or wealthy Victorian-era philanthropists. And it means that Boomer activists have a loudness

PROPERTY APARTHEID AND THE BOOMER CREDIBILITY GAP

and self-importance about them rather like a car alarm – hated and really disruptive to the neighbourhood. Everything has to be about them. If it's not about them it's about someone they know, knew or watched on TV.

But it's Boomer suburbanites, your Kath and your Kel, who are the majority. They are usually conservative, materialistic and insular. There is a reason why Tom and Barbara Good from *The Good Life* were thought to be weird – because they were. They were a world away from the slavish brand loyalty of Boomer suburbia that generations of advertisers have relied on since the Boomers got pocket money.

Whatever their subset, Boomers are intent on keeping control. Erica Lewis could barely contain her anger when talking to me about this breed. 'At the moment I certainly feel that I am being set up to be sucked dry by a generation that won't look after me. As a theory, making it better for the next generation seems to have died in the arse.'

If city-living Boomers weren't such caricatures it would be easier to dismiss generalisations about them. But when you watch these people treat multiculturalism as an eating strategy and sign petitions against freeways and then petitions against a proposed block of flats down the road that, if built, would mean the freeways for commuters wouldn't be necessary, it's hard not to be cynical.

As the first teenagers the Boomers decided to copyright that personality. They are still trying to be 'young' in their fifties and sixties and 'they seem shocked their stranglehold on youth culture is waning'.[6] They complain about their children still living at home in their twenties – not growing up – and then give newspapers interviews about the joys of rock concerts and tantric yoga at 60. Hello? You're not Eddie from *Ab Fab*. And if you are you should be embarrassed.

The lie of the crazy free love '60s continues to grate. The truth is less glamorous: 'Most young Australians in the '60s and early '70s

PLEASE JUST F* OFF . . . IT'S OUR TURN NOW

21st century feminism

There's a lot of older feminists who don't actually get politics, they would struggle to remember the cross-benchers on a bad day . . . They think that the justice of the argument will win it . . . I think we understand that it's not about being right, it's about having the numbers.

Erica Lewis, 29

Baby Boomer feminists are as tough as nails. They have their career and nothing else. They think that women our age should have that as well and they don't understand we want more balanced lifestyles. My boss was so unsympathetic and had such a limited understanding of anyone else's choices. When I asked to take unpaid leave to go overseas and travel she was like 'Why? Why?' We've had all this feminism and we're meant to be able to have what we want but they're like – 'you can only have what we wanted'. I want so much more than a career and not a career at the cost of everything else.

Tammy Ingold, 25

The most irritating thing about the 'second wave' (of feminists) is their attitude towards young women today. We are constantly being told we don't care, and that the regression of the women's struggle is our fault . . . Just because things may not be done in the same way as 20 to 30 years ago, shouldn't render new strategies and alliances and tactics completely invisible to the older generation.

Anna York, 25

I tend to think feminism is about acknowledging that men and women grow up differently . . . Being a feminist is about

> acknowledging the difference and figuring out how to negotiate that in the most empowering way.
>
> *Rachel Hills, 23*

> I hate them (boomer feminists) . . . I think they've created a glass ceiling for women. But it's not glass, it's a wooden ceiling. I was in Year 12 the year they brought in the 35 percent quota in the ALP – here I was thinking I want to get into politics and that this is good, and then I looked and realised all the women were in their forties and fifties using it for their own power base, not mentoring me . . . it's like 'operate within our boundaries or fuck off'.
>
> *Kate Pasterfield, 27*

> I look back at Eva Cox flitting back and forth between jobs as she needed to fund her activism and think we would never be employed again if we acted like that. We can't behave the way some of the 60s and 70s radicals did – largely because of policies they created when elected to government.
>
> *Erica Lewis, 29*

left school at 16 to get blue-collar and clerical jobs and, like their parents, raised their kids in the suburbs.'[7] Remember the myth of the '60s protest era? 'Even in 1969, when protest was at a height, the president of the SRC, Percy Allan, estimated that radical activists numbered just two percent of the student body, their followers 25 percent.'[8]

The author of *Gangland*, Mark Davis, agrees. 'Forget "free love" and Woodstock,' he writes, 'the enduring legacy of the Boomers is economic rationalism.' The majority, of course, just got drunk, got laid and moved to the suburbs. It's not exactly *Forrest Gump* is it?

But what can you expect from the original and best 'on-message generation'? You might think it's not possible to present a generation as a homogenous group of people – but it's been happening for 30 years. Boomer history is as familiar as home to me and that's scary. We were encouraged to follow rather than learn from them. But they've simply invented new traditions. They make you feel bad if you don't want to copy them. And when you do, they criticise you for not being original.

Boomer social movements

Let's be clear that Boomer activists created important platforms for social change. However, the majority are more socially conservative than my generation and their activist elite have fixed and limited understandings of how to make a difference in 21st-century public affairs, as the Iraq marches demonstrated.

A closer examination of Boomer-era activist movements is as revealing as those marches. In *Play Power*, Richard Neville says the Vietnam War acted as 'one Great Youth Unifier'. If opinion polling had been in full swing at the time, that statement would not have held up. Unfortunately my generation doesn't have the luxury of escaping such scrutiny. We just get to flounder without a narrative.

But if Richard Neville can pass off hazy memories as history in Australia, the Brits didn't let him get away with it. Far from taking London by storm as he and his acolytes would have us believe, Neville and co 'generated enough hot air to launch Hindenburg II'.[9] *Private Eye* said of Neville's book, *Play Power*: 'the human story of a young Australian who comes to London and finds happiness by bringing out the worst magazine in the history of the world.'

In hindsight, the Boomer social movements were severely limited in scope. These movements thought they were radically changing the world, but most only changed legislation and the lifestyles of the participants. Boomers also created self-serving elites amongst the minorities they purported to liberate, and turned around and led them. Engage corporations in social change? Are you kidding?

The rebellion was most often individual and non-political, expressed through consumer tastes in music and in symbolism ... a reaction against the affluent boredom of overly comfortable adolescence.[10]

The Estate we're in

There is one issue so inextricably linked to this generation that it deserves more scrutiny. It screams out 'hypocrisy' louder than a shiny new billboard for a gated community. The issue is property.

You don't need a brain to succeed in Australia, only property. Why people still bother going to university is a mystery — it clearly delivers lower returns than property investment. Indeed, the mental attitudes underpinning our property market culture have much in common with psychological disorders. Indeed, the greed-fuelled trajectory of our recent property market could be viewed as thinly disguised kleptomania. Just look at the type of headlines ('Stamp out Stamp Duty', 'Taxed to Death') that fill the newspapers at the mere suggestion of anything getting in the way of making a killing. Young people are losing the chance at a plot of land and the nation is losing the plot in tandem. Cheaper housing is something that should be celebrated — not flagged up as the first step towards National Emergency. Yet these ideas are not even on the horizon of the smug twice-mortgaged — they're too busy calling their agent about the 'two bedroom plus study' that just went on the market in *Horizon*.

Australian house prices have risen by 110 percent, on average, between 1997 and 2004. In Germany they fell by three percent, while the US, Italy and France recorded rises of roughly 60 percent. Indeed 'never before have house prices risen so fast in real terms'.[11] In Australia the ratio of average house prices to rents or incomes is between 40 and 60 percent higher than its long-term average and JP Morgan estimates that house prices nationally are overvalued by 22 percent.[12] In *Seachange* Bob Jellie remarked, 'What's the one thing that unites all? ... Real estate. Everyone believes in property.' He got

PLEASE JUST F* OFF . . . IT'S OUR TURN NOW

the mood right, but property doesn't unite us anymore — it divides the generations. It is Property Apartheid.

The date: April 24, 2004. The time: 9 p.m. The location: a dark Lebanese restaurant on inner Sydney's Cleveland Street. The players: a bunch of twenty-somethings you've never heard of. The reason: who cares? Here, I finally lost my sense of proportion about property. I sat down chewing the fat with friends about where we would be in five years and it emerged that only one of us believed they would have a mortgage. If the dodgy air-conditioning unit had yet to send a chill down my spine, this did. Then my friends scrunched up their faces at the idea of banding together to buy an investment property — on the basis that they couldn't afford to. My parents owned a terrace in Newtown outright at that age! After starting from scratch! Without a degree between them!

There is a distinct bloc of people who possess property and with it, wealth. This begets further wealth and property, beyond the proportion to which they are entitled. And it's not us. More than three-quarters of Boomers own a home — worth an average $231,000 to each individual boomer — and they control 37 percent of national wealth.[13] Only 52 percent of Generation X is paying off a home and 39 percent still rent — they control just 19 percent of national wealth, despite outnumbering the Boomers. Generation Y controls just one percent of national wealth.

Try to raise the issue of their disproportionate wealth and power with a Boomer and you get a response articulated at the level of *Little Britain*'s Vikki Pollard — 'yeah, but no, but, yeah, but no'. Watch them descend from confusion to apoplexy. If you are lucky they may even throw you on to an unrelated tangent, like blaming their children for still living at home in their twenties.

The National Centre for Social and Economic Modelling (NATSEM) released a report in 2003 — *Generation Xcluded* — confirming that between 1989 and 1999 those aged 25–39 saw their share of national wealth drop by 10 percent. The conclusion: many young people are now 'locked out' of the property market, possibly permanently. This issue is important because wealth that is savings- and asset-based is distributed far more unequally than income, and the income inequality gap is already growing. Matthew Taylor, former UK think-tank guru and head of policy at Downing Street, wrote in *New Statesmen* in 2002:

> People with assets feel more secure and able to plan for the future. In a world increasingly characterised by change, wealth can help cope with unexpected life events. It allows people to meet the lumpy costs often associated with transitional stages.

Or as a young Sydneysider Rhys Weekly explained to the Australian Senate:

> I don't believe it is unfair for me to aim for a similar quality of life to that my parents had. My expectations don't reach to owning a waterfront property. I just want to be able to ensure a reasonable quality of life for myself and my family . . .

What we are dealing with (or not dealing with) is a structural and organised inequity. The people who perpetuate the inequity are either consciously greedy or hypnotised by the state-sponsored rhetoric that property is a holy grail. We can expect nothing less from a generation who have spent their whole lives being property trendsetters. From suburban childhood utopias, to inner-city gentrification, to *Seachange* shacks, to empty-nest city apartments, to the original McMansions, these people have displayed a lust for property that makes them fitting conquerors of the throbbing oligarchical property market that calls Australia home.

Investing in property for financial gain is especially attractive in Australia because the tax advantages of negative gearing make it an excuse to top up more sustainable but less attractive forms of saving.

If you're an investor who makes $20,000 a year in rental income, and has $30,000 in mortgage and other expenses, you get a tax deduction of $10,000 and pay only 24 percent capital gains tax when you sell the place, instead of the 48.5 percent you'd pay on ordinary income.[14]

Even when a state introduces new property taxes, as NSW did in 2004, they get abolished the next year under pressure from alleged 'Mum and Dad' investors.

Capital Gains Tax on property at a paltry 24.25 percent is madness. You get taxed twice as much to work and do something useful as you do sitting about speculating and economically enslaving young Australians as a result. The cut in Capital Gains Tax was made in 1999 – and, surprise, surprise, that's when our latest obsession with property prices – according to *The Economist* an 'extraordinary and potentially dangerous property binge' – went into overdrive.[15]

This is just one example of how current attitudes to property are a systemic problem. This is not a coincidence. It is this very systematic nature of the problem that led the Office of the Deputy Prime Minister in the UK to describe the situation there as 'property apartheid' in 2004. The same week there was an opinion piece in the *Sydney Morning Herald* headlined, 'It's the folk's fault the kids can't move out'. The Profile found 50 percent of 20- to 24-year-olds still live at home, allegedly costing their parents an average $322 a week. (Nonsense, of course. If that were really the case then the parents could boot their children out, pay more than half of the kids mortgages, get their lives back and still come out with change.)

Whatever the real cost, Dominic Knight was right when he addressed Boomers with this ultimatum: '... perhaps you'd rather your precious housing market crashed so we kids could afford to rent or buy somewhere east of the Blue Mountains? Didn't think so.'[16]

Of course, it's not that society doesn't expect individual acts of altruism from its members. As recently as February 2005 young people were again called on to make personal sacrifices to fix the 'dental health crisis' – by moving to the middle of nowhere for two years after graduation to fill dentist shortages.[17] As with other professions such as teaching, here young people are simply expected to put up with this as some kind of penance or initiation. Put the boot on the other foot and ask Boomers to sell their properties cheaply or stay out of the investment property game and you'd be laughed out of town, if not slapped across the face.

At the height of our property fever in 2002 the annual growth rate in property prices hit 19.2 percent in Sydney according to the Australian Bureau of Statistics. In 2003 Brisbane faced an exponential 31.1 percent rise. What does that mean tangibly? A mid-level office worker, for example, who bought a house in a middle-class Sydney suburb for $AU188,000 in 1996 was offered $AU720,000 in 2003. In 2005 it takes 500 weeks of average wages to buy a typical home, compared to 350 weeks in the US.[18] In Sydney's beachside Clovelly you'll pay $1.1–3 million to own an old, falling-apart three-bedroom home. Apartments can't be found for under $530,000. All this to live in a Labor-voting suburb, which, let's face it, has a concrete-edged little beach and few shops or restaurants. A three-bedroom house in grotty industrial Mascot goes for $732,500. The median house price in Bondi is $1.05 million. In the words of Mora Main, the Chairwoman of the Waverley Council Development Control Committee, Sydney's beachside suburbs are becoming 'an unsustainable monoculture of the wealthy,' and the crisis is 'acute'.[19]

This is property-driven social polarisation – a renovated version of the divisions between garden and slum suburbs a century ago. There are now so many class-cleansed suburbs, gated communities, ghetto areas and large-scale rather than integrated housing commission estates that Property Apartheid is apparent to anyone who bothers to look.

How people acquire wealth matters. Massive wealth gains based on acts like property speculation are unjust because they are unrelated to skill and merit. We must ask ourselves whether it really is OK to acquire wealth from owning multiple investment properties in the same small market. The answer, I fear, is no.

Property rights are the foundation of capitalism, but the concept of private property is also a social institution. That means the owners of private property are trustees as well as creditors of the nation. It is this principle that makes it unfair to lock good capitalists like my generation out of the property party. It's not good for capitalism and it's not good for us. Blind greed has pushed our property market into dysfunction and there's only one generation you can point your finger at.

In 2006 under the cold, harsh fluorescent light of the wrath of the Reserve Bank of Australia it's obvious this madness cannot go on. Commentators described the Reserve Bank's 2005 criticisms of our property mindset 'as bold an ultimatum as a central banker has ever sent to Canberra'. According to the seers, 'the Goldilocks years are over'.[20] Instead of stupid tax breaks to favour property investment by the already-wealthy we need investment in productive businesses.[21]

It's a game a few brave souls had been trying to play in NSW in April 2004. Then the NSW Government changed its property tax regime and even *The Daily Telegraph* acknowledged the gravity of that decision from that most cautious of governments:

> Until yesterday Bob Carr faced the unpalatable prospect of going down in history as the Labor Premier who has sat on his hands and done nothing while an entire generation of kids were priced out of home ownership...[22]

To fill the non-Sydney, non-property obsessed readership in: the NSW Government's 'First Home Plus' program was changed so that first-home buyers purchasing property under $500,000 would no longer be charged stamp duty (saving up to $18,000) while sales of investment properties would be hit with a 2.25 percent exit stamp duty (the Vendor Duty Tax) as well as entry stamp duty – all to discourage the rich and upwardly greedy from overheating the property market by shuffling properties between themselves for higher and higher prices. In its first nine months the policy helped 31,897 first-home buyers into the market.[23] It is also disappointed a few people and led them to buy their overpriced shithouse apartments in other states.

Annette Sampson's analysis in *The Sydney Morning Herald* was devastating: 'For the one-in-10 Boomers who have become landlords in recent years, the changes represent a wholesale movement of the goalposts at a time when they are already faced with low rental returns and muted prospects of capital growth.' Heart-wrenching stuff. The freakishly selfish bastards were still banging on about it in 2005, backed by the NSW Property Council, and eventually got their way.[24]

In the words of the then NSW Treasurer himself: 'An overheated property market is only good for people like me – people who, besides owning their own home, have made profits by owning an investment or second property ... it's no good for the community and it's certainly no good for young people.'[25] But just a year later the NSW Labor Government lost its political guts in what it spun as a democratic response to grassroots concerns, and reversed the property entry tax changes in favour of new insurance duties. From the Fairfax media came equally acidic assessments:

> FAIR to whom? To western suburbs battlers doing it so tough they can afford holiday homes and smarties who thought the way to 'save' was to speculate on negatively geared rental apartments. Who will be paying the higher insurance duty? All those filthy rich people who insure their house and contents. If this is Labor's idea of fairness, it just shows how far it's strayed from its ideals.
>
> *Ross Gittins*

PLEASE JUST F* OFF . . . IT'S OUR TURN NOW

> STAKING your fortune, or even your retirement income, on escalating real estate values and favourable rezonings is a gamble, not a birthright.
>
> *Adele Horin*[26]

The lesson from this orgy of the politically pathetic is never get between a Baby Boomer and the property market. So much for the generational change represented by Morris Iemma's replacement of Bob Carr as Premier.

Expensive and scarce housing helps no one. And we can fix that now by being honest about it or we can look forward to a world where governments force recalcitrant people into line. Do you fancy driving past billboards that read: 'WARNING: Baby Boomers buying property in this area', and messages on 'For Sale' signs explaining 'Your investment property strategy harms others'. No, I thought not. You can't have one generation getting a free bonanza via property (after also going to uni for free) and then have another paying for the most basic of public services, paying through the nose for education and not being able to afford a home without resentment being generated.

IF we create market universities run purely on market principles they may be of their age, but they will not be able to transcend it.
Fredico Mayer, UNESCO Director 1997 [1]

WHAT is the point of spending thousands a year to send your children to lavishly appointed private schools when they graduate to crumbling universities?
Adele Horin [2]

WE can't really call ourselves a public university anymore, when only 23 percent of our income is directly guaranteed by the Federal Government.
Professor Glyn Davis,
Vice Chancellor, University of Melbourne

CHAPTER SEVEN

Generation HECS and the slow death of public education

The legacy of Generation HECS

The Higher Education Contribution Scheme, or HECS, is a sleeping giant of Australian public policy and daily life. It's not a government-changing policy, evidently, and people generally accept it because the principle is hard to argue with and they see no alternative. It's the practice that's the problem. Aside from weighing down the spending, credit ratings and expectations of more than a million Australians at any given time (closer to two million when those who've paid off their HECS debts are counted) it is also that rare breed of public policy – one destined to intrinsically piss off more people the longer it exists. The number of people with HECS debts grows every time a student enrols, every year, and people do not forget massive debt easily.

If the growth in annual HECS fees per student over the first 15 years of HECS is repeated in the next 15 (it has shot up 800 percent over that period), by 2020 the highest HECS rate will have breached $50,000 a year. The government, who made so much of their 'debt

Generation HECS Snapshots

I feel bad for kids who have to pay their way through uni – obviously you can't concentrate all the time and it's a lot more stressful.

Paula Fong, 22, Darwin

I wouldn't have done my masters if my work hadn't paid for 75 percent of it.

Simon Palagyi, 27, Sydney

I am reluctant to publicise the atrocity of the educational standards here because it essentially devalues my degree.

Jean, international student[3]

Hypocritical uni management – who are all boomers – will justify whatever crap policy with the 'you don't understand how hard the Howard Government has made things for us' line. It's a cover. They're hypocrites. They have this 'I was radical in my day' line, but now it's OK to cop-out. I'd like to think I have a more sustainable approach, where I am still going to act in the interests of others when I'm 50.

Former University Council member, Flinders University

truck' in the 1996 election campaign have simply managed to privatise that debt – we're all driving own our debt trucks now.

Thousands of women, and a few men, will go to their grave with a HECS debt. And that says it all, really. Recite all the fancy economic justifications you like – there is something morally wrong about a situation where a government set up to serve your interests can saddle you with a debt that you will never fully repay. The government says 'we value your contribution to society *so* much that we will make you pay for it until you have decomposed'. Thanks.

PLEASE JUST F* OFF . . . IT'S OUR TURN NOW

Or you could view HECS in terms of documents like Peter Costello's Inter-Generational Report, as one of my interview subjects did:

> It's lunacy – they want everyone to have a better education to be a better educated society so we can all have higher paid jobs so we pay more taxes to give old people who had free education more pensions, but they then say 'we're not going to spend any more on education, we're going to make you pay for it', so you're still paying for it in 20 years.

I could only pity one friend who burst into tears when her employer admitted they had forgotten to deduct her HECS contribution from her wages one financial year – leaving her with a lump sum of $3,000 to repay to the Australian Tax Office. If you spread the payments you're hit with compound interest. (And they say HECS is indexed to inflation.)

HECS is unlike other debt. Your HECS debt isn't stuck on the university enrolment form like a price tag. You don't have to hand over a credit card. Most galling of all, when you find yourself sitting on the concrete floor of a 1970s lecture theatre, or physically locked out of your very first lecture as 160 UTS Financial Markets students did in 2000 because there were no seats and it was a fire hazard, you have no right to exchange or refund. The fees can be put up arbitrarily with no compensation in quality. There is no consumer watchdog. If there is a market in education it is a dysfunctional, crippled beast and HECS spreads through it like a cancer.

Even if you believe in the principle of user pays you should ask why it isn't applied more widely? How many times do we have to watch farmers complain about another (shock, horror) drought and receive 'drought assistance' (i.e. hand-outs) in return? When they introduce HECS for farmers then I'll shut up.

Despite all the alluring analogies about education as a market and the righteousness of individual contributions from students to match

GENERATION HECS AND THE SLOW DEATH OF PUBLIC EDUCATION

their individual gain from a degree, it's a lie. In what other market do the prices rise 800 percent at the same time as the quality stays the same and the number of items on sale increases? MBAs breed like rabbits did before myxomatosis and the labour market is now saturated with degree holders that are devaluing your degree by their very existence. That's life – except the fees still rise.

Indeed, 23 overseas students were thrown out of the country in 2003–4 for being engaged unlawfully in the sex industry because they needed the money.[4] A ministerial spokesman said these people were in the industry because they were 'simply trying to earn extra cash'. Doesn't it make you proud to be Australian?

The cultural manifestations of HECS are pointed to by the functioning markets that surround it. A recent marketing tactic of pubs that surround university zones is to run trivia and bingo-style competitions advertised as opportunities for students to 'win their HECS'.

You can walk past the posters advertising this competition if you walk against the crowds one morning as they break the banks of Redfern station and surge towards Sydney University. In their thousands they squeeze their way along the narrow dirty streets to take up their jealously guarded HECS places (tens of thousands miss out these days; there's no better way to make people grateful for the crap they end up with). Nervous geeks, over-stylised *Cosmo* readers, the determined and focused first-generation Australians, the part-time students late because they've just dropped the kids off at school or childcare, and the academic types in black jeans who look like they have just entered the 1980s. Interesting, diverse, determined. These are not the faces of protest and revolt. There are not many lefty student radicals here.

PLEASE JUST F* OFF . . . IT'S OUR TURN NOW

A HECS on student activism

In the 1970s we were led to believe things were different. 'Life was exciting, I wanted to push more boundaries and see what happened. I felt so purposeful, I felt as though I was going to change the world.'[5]

Today's students are behaving themselves because they can't afford not to. Being more diverse, over worked, more indebted than those before them, it is even less surprising that these students don't mobilise behind one position or one campaign. Yet that is somehow disappointing to the arbiters of our culture.

I often think many people view students as they would their own book collections. They create book collections to reflect the type of person they want to be, rather than who they are. As a society we want students to be a bit noisy because we want a better world and it makes us feel better to think that someone is out there creating it – that someone is taking care of all *that* while we do nothing. The media want students for some colour and movement and because protest is part of the cultural furniture – any serious investigation of student issues breaches that niche, however, and is therefore avoided.

Bemoaning that students 'just aren't idealistic like they used to be' is not only incorrect; it's shorthand for blaming them for the policies that make their lives difficult and indebted. It allows older people to wash their hands of responsibility for the mess their generation has put universities in, which is very different to the legacy their parents left them, as anonymous quotes in Alison Pressley's book *Living in the 70s* makes all too clear:

> The brilliant thing was that Whitlam made tertiary education free, so suddenly I could go to university. That was a major social change and it really helped the energy of the time.

> I went to university because it was free and I got a scholarship.

GENERATION HECS AND THE SLOW DEATH OF PUBLIC EDUCATION

I don't remember feeling a whole lot of pressure.

I've watched how much less fun university has become over the years.'

My parents were adamant I should go into the armed forces so I could get a degree for free (yes, the government will pay for your education if you are happy to be cannon fodder) or to stay in my home town of Coffs Harbour and do a degree I had no interest in, to reduce living costs. The message was true for my family when HECS was barely $2,000 a year in the mid-90s, and it remains true now that HECS is more likely $5,000 a year: people fear HECS.

> IF you're at uni and you're losing money there is much greater pressure to get in and out as fast as possible . . . Activism is one of the casualties of that.
>
> *Daney, 25, Sydney*

Today, even student politicians have to be professionals just to get anything done. One can't just be slightly interested or merely able to spare a couple of hours. To hold a representative position in student politics in the 21st century usually requires taking a 'leave of absence' from your studies and becoming a hack. I know because that's exactly what I did. We have slick, sophisticated student politicians today but not many will be able to cope with the massive challenge of reviving interest in parliamentary politics. Without remedial action their extended half-life at the helm of our public institutions will irradiate our politics over the next 20 years like some kind of terrible nuclear accident.

> Student politics actively knocks out of you the emotional literacy and disdain for the time-wasting and 'scheming', that characterise the truly popular and effective politicians of our age. It is awful for those wasting

so much energy in the best years of their life, but the sad truth is that the good student politician makes a lousy real politician.[8]

Thanks to the pressures HECS puts on most students the political elites nursed by the student political system came from an even smaller gene pool that the general elites produced by university. We will all be poorer for it.

HECS sums don't add up

Means-tested systems, whatever their target audience, are always expensive to administer because you have to work hard at keeping people out and identifying the lucky members of whatever little welfare club is going. And when it comes to an investment like tertiary education the costs of administering the system – borne by government, universities and families alike – are exposed as absurd. But forget the rhetoric; let's just look at the cold, hard figures.

How the hell does the government calculate that it costs, say $10,000 or $12,000 per year per student to be taught a university course, anyway? My undergraduate university course at the University of Technology in Sydney had a full-time course load of eight hours per week of classes. There are 12 weeks of compulsory classes at UTS for two semesters a year. No special equipment was needed or provided. Generally there were no extra costs like replacing tutors if they were sick or unavailable. I didn't study in a new building, except the university library, so I presumably wasn't being charged much for the cost of infrastructure. There were no examination costs because there were no exams – it was all coursework assessment. I paid for all my own textbooks and photocopied 'readers' (sets of articles to be read between classes). I paid for printing at computer rooms and for replacement student cards and copies of my academic transcript for job interviews ($25 for three pages of A4). If I'd attended all the classes I would have spent a total of 192 hours per year at university

– about what most people spend doing a month's work – for a course that was harder to get into than most medical degrees. For those 192 hours I was charged $3,768 (it increases) every year. If I was to start studying under most recent changes to HECS in 2004 that figure goes up to $7,854 for some courses. All this means I paid $20 per hour to attend university, which, according to the mainstream rhetoric, is only 30–50 percent of the cost of educating me.

It's true that older universities with the asset base and bigger income streams can accommodate extra students more cheaply. New universities will always shift the cost of their new buildings and other infrastructure on to students because they never receive enough in capital grants from the government to cover these costs. However, using the figures most often used in public debate, believing that HECS is right and fair therefore means you must accept the proposition that it costs a whopping $40–$70 an hour to have me sitting in a room with up to 400 other people for lectures and 30 other people for tutorials. It makes me wonder why I don't just ask the government for vouchers to the nearest reflexology and massage centre where I could at least do my reading in comfort. The government would save money doing that if their current figures are correct.

I make no suggestion that this assessment represents hole-proof accounting – I am not an accountant. All I suggest is that having thought about this quite a lot I see no way to explain the figures used to create the impression that the 700,000-odd people who are university students at any given time are 'middle class welfare recipients'. It pisses me off to be taken for such a fool.

Women and HECS

IF you think about HECS and do the statistical averages using the figures that show women earn less . . . and you consider HECS indexes regardless of whether you are in

PLEASE JUST F* OFF . . . IT'S OUR TURN NOW

> the workforce or not, then you see a woman's HECS bill is ultimately larger. Women statistically will pay more for their education than the men they sit next to in class.
>
> *Erica Lewis, 29, Canberra*

The estimates of how many women will die without paying their HECS back in full are as high as two in five.[6] This is an appalling possibility. Appalling in the same way that politicians chorus about raising the birth rate but do nothing about the reasons for its decline. Children are already very expensive – and with the 2004 changes to HECS they just got 30 percent more expensive. If you consider that raising a child might cost a family roughly $200 per week, and that six percent HECS repayments on weekly wages of $1,000 are $60, then that bumps up those expenses to about $260 or $320 a week depending on your exact income and whether one or both parents have a HECS debt. That would leave you barely $400 a week for a mortgage (yeah, right) and everything else that two people must purchase to get by. Even using a sole parent with the full after-tax income of the two-parent family as an example, the extra childcare costs wipe out their income advantage. If you are trying to balance all that in a capital city there is one word for you – screwed. Could it be that HECS is affecting the fertility rate, or delaying childbirth? But let's be even blunter: the situation women are stuck in with HECS is actually a Federal Budget Black Hole.

> TWO out of every five women are never going to repay their debt. Especially alarming given more and more women are going to uni – this means a massive amount of money that is on the books as coming back (accrual accounting) will not actually come back. In New Zealand they had to write off about one billion dollars of debt two years ago.
>
> *Daniel Kyriacou, 2003 NUS President*

You won't read about that in the newspaper.

HECS encourages under-investment in undergraduate education

At the same time as we should be exponentially increasing government contributions to all levels of education from early childhood through to university, we have allowed HECS to become an excuse to cease non-fee investment in undergraduate education. From Adele Horin to Rupert Murdoch ('it is no exaggeration to say we are threatened with global irrelevance') a broad spectrum agrees: Australian undergraduate education is so under-funded it's a joke. Universities live with the illusion that the HECS money will plug the biggest gaps in their budgets and they hope no one notices the rest.

Here is the best example of the education market 'functioning'. Universities run more and more of the cheapest subjects. These are the ones that are shallow and which anyone can do. If it's too hard to manufacture new shallow subjects a university will just make deep subjects shallow by merging three or four of them. I used to sit in classes where the tutors couldn't even remember the various subjects the students were enrolled in. Huh? As a second-year student I might be doing Comparative Social Change, but there would also be a post-graduate in the room doing a subject with a different name, which would give them different credit points and for which they would hand in a different assessment. All from the same teaching material and sometimes based on group-work! Then again, it's far more likely these days that you will be shifted into a 'placement' as a subject. Vocational? Yes. Extremely cheap? Double yes.

Then there is 'Vice-Chancellor's week' (well, two of them actually). This is where everyone gets a week off class so the university can turn off the lights and skip paying its casual teaching staff. The official reason is that this is when the Vice-Chancellor's get together for a retreat to plan for the sector. I don't think anyone believes we all stop work to pay homage as though they are ancient gods. It's all about the cash.

Yet what cash does HECS bring in relative to the whole university sector budget? The pointlessness of the 2004 HECS increases is obvious just by looking to the example of one major university. Melbourne University decided to increase fees by the maximum 25 percent allowed. The HECS increase will raise just $5.4 million a year, yet the university has a gross annual income of over one billion dollars. That's a lot of pain for little gain.

Corporations getting a free ride

We are continually told that students must contribute to their education because their degrees accord them individual benefits. At a surface level this principle is unarguable (except for the fact that through high marginal income tax rates these graduates will subsidise future generations for the rest of their lives). There is, however, an extraordinary lack of attention paid to the contribution of that other great direct beneficiary of higher education – the corporate sector. Do they not derive a benefit from the higher skills and critical analysis of their graduate employees? Do they not save money from outsourcing their own in-house training to the university post-graduate and short course market? Do they not make squillions by poaching university researchers and commercialising their work? We know they receive all these benefits yet we fob off the public policy challenge of finding a way to make them contribute. It's easier to lie to ourselves and pretend that HECS will fund everything.

Career detours

HECS certainly affects the distribution of skills and people across the labour market. Knowing that they will leave university with a large debt deters some students from taking the courses they would enjoy and be good at, in favour of courses that will lead to higher incomes.

'Students are often studying in one area and working in another to keep their options open,' Johanna Wyn, University of Melbourne Youth Research Centre director told the *Gold Coast Bulletin* in February 2004. Translation: students often don't think they'll get a return on their HECS investment so they just use their degree as insurance against their self-made first attempts at success.

Fuelling the debt addiction

> THE biggest thing is how much we accept debt today – we live on credit. We live entirely off money that we borrow which informs a certain state of mind about debt, and HECS is just part of that. Our parents get very stressed about interest, we don't.
>
> *Rose Tracey, 1998 National Union of Students President*

Knowing I would be left with a debt when I left university simply encouraged me to apply for credit cards while I was at university. I never expected to live a debt-free life and I wasn't prepared to have a crap life for four years while others around me enjoyed their alleged best years. I did the sums and realised that making minimum payments on a series of credit cards was a sustainable way to get a better lifestyle quickly. My credit card debt was never greater than my HECS debt. Put another way 'I'm not going to live a pov (poor) life just because of the stupid policies of the Howard Government,' says Nicole Tschaut a 22-year-old from Brisbane. Alternatively you put up with it for a while but then don't go back for postgraduate study when you should or could:

> MOST people who are paying $120 a fortnight in HECS repayments really say: 'I am not going to go back, I want to pay this off and not get any more debt.'
>
> *Sam, 29, Sydney*

It seems you can tell people everything they should know about credit, but when they see a completely different attitude from government – 'To be in debt is glorious' – the message will be set aside. This is another legacy of HECS.

HECS and the strangling of public ideas

The voices that make it into the leading streams of public debate on more than a one-off basis are inherently those of the elite. It's a privilege to be able to talk to or write for millions of people at a time. But every society needs an elite to encourage the consideration of the big issues of the time, to 'offer specialised knowledge and expertise for the greater good' as 'Civic-minded people willing to master detail' according to Mark Davis.[7] But our universities and education policies are not allowing the space in which to develop these civic-minded ideas. Australians finish their degrees much quicker than Europeans, and without the generalist courses that are mandatory in the good US universities – this reduces our capacity to be innovative. Coupled with the new unfair financial pressures that most students face, we are being to create an elite based on 'who can pay for what' rather than on 'merit'. We already have a small gene pool in Australia and it is sheer madness to filter kids out of it because they can't cope with working 30 hours a week whilst also studying medicine. That's not going to help us punch above our weight in a competitive global economy, is it?

Regardless of where our elite is or should be coming from, an equally worrying fact is that universities themselves are not producing any new elites at all. Why? Because we now have a generational closed shop when it comes to academia. Tenure isn't just about academic freedom anymore – it's about generational inequity and saving second-rate academics from themselves while denying better young academics chances the second-raters have had for decades. With no new voices and no investment in the development of new ideas, it is perhaps unsurprising that Australian public debate is so stale.

HECS and the economy

Sucking $120 a fortnight from hundreds of thousands of people into a government black hole obviously dampens consumer demand. In their submission to the Nelson Review the Real Estate Institute even expressed a fear that this may even extend to the housing market as banks begin to ask about HECS debts when assessing suitability for loans. At a lower level the fact that HECS debts often mean one's liabilities outstrip one's assets could be having a disastrous effect on individual credit ratings. We don't know because no one has done the research. The Business Council of Australia has also raised concerns about the $14 billion Australians now owe in HECS. NATSEM aired similar problems in their 2003 report *Generation Xcluded*. Think of what a boost to the economy this would be if the debt was wiped out. This is money that would otherwise be in the private sector.

When does HECS cease to be HECS?

For tens of thousands of students, until July 2004, HECS was never a deferred payment. Because they worked 25 hours a week or more, they would breach the HECS repayment threshold which had hovered just above $20,000 since 1997 (after being cut from the old policy of average male weekly earnings under Labor). The truly welcome change in Brendan Nelson's review of higher education conducted in 2003 and 2004 is surely the lifting of this repayment threshold. It should be noted, however, that only in 2008 will the threshold reach the reasonable level of $36,000. If the existing policy had remained in place the threshold would have been $31,000 by that time. By 2008 average male weekly earnings will be $50,000 or more.

It wasn't the radical change we need, just clever politics in the face of a wimpish Labor education policy.

HECS encouraging people to flee Australia

More than a million Australians are now living overseas (discussed in more detail in Generation eXpat) and for some HECS keeps them there – if you aren't earning in Australia the Tax Office can't make you pay it back.

> MY HECS debt is certainly a significant factor in deciding where I am financially better off . . . the Australian lifestyle and climate will eventually bring me back, probably when we decide to start a family. By then I will have spent many of my most productive, innovative and tax-paying years elsewhere.
>
> *Kenneth Scott Mackenzie, London*

> I have come to the conclusion that Australia is nothing more than a suburban backwater in the middle of nowhere . . . If an expat has a highly-paid and successful career overseas there is no incentive to go home. Most likely you will return to a lesser job, pay higher taxes if you earn too much and not to mention a HECS debt you cannot jump over . . .
>
> *Lisa Stoneham, Patterson Lakes, Victoria*

It's pretty sad when a government policy is even in the frame when your most talented people weigh up whether they can bear to remain in their own country. It's pretty sad when political parties are too timid to acknowledge what every parent, every ambitious teenager and the country's most respected economics group, Access Economics, knows to be true:

Education is increasingly becoming the 'engine room' of modern economies. If we get this part of the economy right, most other things ought to fall into place (or be better placed), because increased investment in education boosts both productivity and participation.[9]

Ten things we hate about HECS

1. You don't get a refund when a class is cancelled.
2. You begin paying it back when earning barely the Federal Award minimum wage.
3. People with dough get a discount for paying it upfront.
4. It deters us from further study after our first degree.
5. The amount of money spent by student unions protesting HECS could rescue a developing nation from bankruptcy.
6. You don't get charged HECS if you are in the armed forces.
7. The Education Ministers who run the policy got their degrees for free.
8. HECS fees seem to increase along exactly the same curve as Vice-Chancellor salary packages and university management international travel budgets.
9. It's a tax! We're supposed to hate tax, remember!
10. It's not even HECS – it's nothing like the original HECS policy.

CHAPTER EIGHT

Corporate slums

Given Nike can have a Vice-President for Corporate Responsibilities and Shell can support the Kyoto Protocol, it makes you wonder when Australian companies are going to stop dragging the chain.[1] But then, hiring a bloke with a heart (yes, you know its going to be a bloke – this is Australia and we don't do executive women) and giving him a shiny name plate isn't going to fix decades of slothfulness. Let's face it – we are in a big corporate hole. We got there by thinking that being relatively free of corruption, having a decent public education system and owning lots of stuff that can be dug up and sold is enough to give us the lifestyle and relatively classless society we want and deserve in the 21st century. It's not.

Activism in the heart of capitalism is not a new fad – Bill Clinton was taking classes on Corporate Social Responsibility at Yale in the early 1970s – but in adopting this cause we are a long way behind other countries and we have the collective misjudgement on the part of '60s and '70s activists who all but ignored corporate activism (it was easier for them to flee to the public sector and academia) to thank for that disadvantage.[2] But enough bitching. These are the rules we should follow:

companies making losses or collapsing. And there's a better than even chance that investors will feel more secure saving and investing if they know competent ethical people are spending their capital. Considering those points it's rather sad, but necessary, for the OECD to propose to tighten its principles of corporate governance.[4] These were rules designed to teach Asia and the former Soviet Union lessons in how proper capitalists do things – now the proper capitalists are being sent back to school! This also demonstrates there's a role for government in these matters: they should be acting as catalysts for change by simply talking about these issues. If they won't lead we need to latch onto the corporate insiders who will. 'Transparency is the best guarantee of good outcomes, outcomes we deserve as citizens and which will underpin our growth as an economy.'[5]

We will know we have embedded this mentality and got ourselves a proper corporate sector when we see more:

- staggered board elections (i.e. when talents beats cliques)
- separated chairperson and chief-executive functions (hello, conflict of interest!)
- senior meetings held if the CEO can't be around (if it can't happen without them, it shouldn't happen at all)
- shareholders electing directors on detailed and independently verifiable information on their skills and recent performance
- negligent directors going to jail.

P.S. the idea that the corporation is a structure that can create profits which individuals can reap but where there is no or little individual responsibility when something goes wrong is repulsive to my generation. It's neither clever nor useful, it's just selfish and unethical. We all live on the same planet, so show some respect. If I walk into a shop and break a plate – I pay for it. If you fuck up a company because you are negligent then you are punished.

- Rule number one: don't listen to anti-capitalists. What a tragic state of being. Go back for a second look if they decide they stand for something.

- Rule number two: Ian Macfarlane's view that 'the nature of a first-rate democratic country' is to have constant economic reform.

- Rule number three: don't listen to those infantile defenders of capitalism who squawk like wind-up dolls that 'corporations only exist to make profits – that is their purpose'. If we wanted Stepford CEOs we'd ask for them.

You can't have a sustainable democracy without a sustainable corporate sector and vice versa. They each require both brains and hearts.

What does that really mean? Nicer companies aren't a panacea to Australia's problems – nice doesn't pay the bills or people's wages – but the price for adhering to the concept of ethics is small. Being decent and ethical is not the precursor to socialist revolution, it's about acknowledging the interconnected world around you. You might say it is a simple matter of conforming to two sets of standards – Corporate Governance (the rules and stated mission of a business) and Corporate Social Responsibility (non-financial accounting, social enterprise and philanthropy). These are practical frameworks that my generation takes seriously, and if you want our money and our labour you will too.

If we are to have capitalism as our economic system then we ought to have capitalism proper – not simply free markets where exploitation, corruption and incorrect pricing are allowed to run the show. In proper capitalism innovation not exploitation is the mark of a successful and forward-thinking investment culture. Transparency rather than mates networks are the guiding principle to business activity. Alongside this, correct pricing – whether brought

> ### 'Not good enough'
>
> In this modern life it's not acceptable that companies and governments don't say what they mean or mean what they say. The rest of us live by those rules – it's time they did too. As she details on **www.notgoodenough.org** Fiona Stewart was trying to get from Brisbane to Melbourne during the Ansett crisis of 2001, with Qantas reaping windfall profits and delivering poor customer service. 'Not fucking good enough' was what she thought and **www.notgoodenough.org** is what she created.
>
> Not Good Enough is an attempt to get to get consumers loud and organised. Ralph Nader without the sanctimony. And they do it with main volunteers spread across Darwin, Queensland and in Melbourne.
>
> 'Gripes listed on the NGE homepage are there for the long haul – until companies catch on and do the big fix, or at least listen. For those who do listen and respond well, their track record will set the industry standards,' promise the NGE team. 'If your supplier/service provider is not matching the winner's standards of business, then think about changing. This will be an evidence based approach to consumer affairs.'
>
> There's a big gap between what Fiona Stewart experienced and the norm in other developed areas. In Europe if your flight is more than two hours late or cancelled you're entitled to several hundred euros compensation or a refund. I'd like to see that in Australia.

about by competition or the inclusion of externalities (like the extra hidden costs of products to the environment and society) – is essential for informed and sustainable consumption. And informed consumption is demanding, discriminating consumption: 'The days of compromise are gone. Customers and consumers want it all: affordability, reliability, security, simplicity, manageability, adaptability, innovation, connection', says Carly Fiorina.

But don't be fooled into thinking millennial buzz-phrases like 'triple-bottom-line accounting' are going to work like a magic wand

– we need to be open to even more radical ideas. A 'triple-bottom line' is still a bottom line. Yet you can't fix outputs with sheer will i you aren't changing inputs as well. We should also be focusing on 'to] line' issues like quality and demand management and investment ii skills. These new approaches need not be divisive, because everyon except lazy fat cats are winners from the process.

Corporate governance

Corporate governance is the way organisations are directed and con trolled; who has rights and responsibilities and what procedures ar used to implement these agreements. It's the flesh on the bones o society's rules for corporations as set out by parliament and publi values systems. Sounds simple, doesn't it? Yet 'the average boarc operates on automatic pilot'.[3]

In some respects it's silly to be surprised at the way we manage t(skip over this whole facet of 21st-century life. Executives never wan regulation or complication to interrupt their business models. The) are hostile to rigorous corporate governance and corporate socia responsibility because these concepts make them think harder and present problems that they used to ignore (or push onto someone else). But we need different rules and more thoughtful business models for thriving in today's different and more difficult environment. And besides, in a joined-up competitive world there is only so long you can ignore reality before other forces make you change your approach.

The 2005 conviction of WorldCom's chief executive Bernie Ebbers of fraud, was a great day for the champions of better corporate governance. That decision said that ignorance was no excuse and that the buck did stop with someone, even in the labyrinth of a major corporation. If that argument applies in the US it certainly applies in Australia.

We would all be better off if the Australian business community took seriously the idea that good corporate governance can prevent

- Rule number one: don't listen to anti-capitalists. What a tragic state of being. Go back for a second look if they decide they stand for something.

- Rule number two: Ian Macfarlane's view that 'the nature of a first-rate democratic country' is to have constant economic reform.

- Rule number three: don't listen to those infantile defenders of capitalism who squawk like wind-up dolls that 'corporations only exist to make profits – that is their purpose'. If we wanted Stepford CEOs we'd ask for them.

You can't have a sustainable democracy without a sustainable corporate sector and vice versa. They each require both brains and hearts.

What does that really mean? Nicer companies aren't a panacea to Australia's problems – nice doesn't pay the bills or people's wages – but the price for adhering to the concept of ethics is small. Being decent and ethical is not the precursor to socialist revolution, it's about acknowledging the interconnected world around you. You might say it is a simple matter of conforming to two sets of standards – Corporate Governance (the rules and stated mission of a business) and Corporate Social Responsibility (non-financial accounting, social enterprise and philanthropy). These are practical frameworks that my generation takes seriously, and if you want our money and our labour you will too.

If we are to have capitalism as our economic system then we ought to have capitalism proper – not simply free markets where exploitation, corruption and incorrect pricing are allowed to run the show. In proper capitalism innovation not exploitation is the mark of a successful and forward-thinking investment culture. Transparency rather than mates networks are the guiding principle to business activity. Alongside this, correct pricing – whether brought

> ### 'Not good enough'
>
> In this modern life it's not acceptable that companies and governments don't say what they mean or mean what they say. The rest of us live by those rules – it's time they did too. As she details on **www.notgoodenough.org** Fiona Stewart was trying to get from Brisbane to Melbourne during the Ansett crisis of 2001, with Qantas reaping windfall profits and delivering poor customer service. 'Not fucking good enough' was what she thought and **www.notgoodenough.org** is what she created.
>
> Not Good Enough is an attempt to get to get consumers loud and organised. Ralph Nader without the sanctimony. And they do it with main volunteers spread across Darwin, Queensland and in Melbourne.
>
> 'Gripes listed on the NGE homepage are there for the long haul – until companies catch on and do the big fix, or at least listen. For those who do listen and respond well, their track record will set the industry standards,' promise the NGE team. 'If your supplier/service provider is not matching the winner's standards of business, then think about changing. This will be an evidence based approach to consumer affairs.'
>
> There's a big gap between what Fiona Stewart experienced and the norm in other developed areas. In Europe if your flight is more than two hours late or cancelled you're entitled to several hundred euros compensation or a refund. I'd like to see that in Australia.

about by competition or the inclusion of externalities (like the extra hidden costs of products to the environment and society) – is essential for informed and sustainable consumption. And informed consumption is demanding, discriminating consumption: 'The days of compromise are gone. Customers and consumers want it all: affordability, reliability, security, simplicity, manageability, adaptability, innovation, connection', says Carly Fiorina.

But don't be fooled into thinking millennial buzz-phrases like 'triple-bottom-line accounting' are going to work like a magic wand

– we need to be open to even more radical ideas. A 'triple-bottom-line' is still a bottom line. Yet you can't fix outputs with sheer will if you aren't changing inputs as well. We should also be focusing on 'top line' issues like quality and demand management and investment in skills. These new approaches need not be divisive, because everyone except lazy fat cats are winners from the process.

Corporate governance

Corporate governance is the way organisations are directed and controlled; who has rights and responsibilities and what procedures are used to implement these agreements. It's the flesh on the bones of society's rules for corporations as set out by parliament and public values systems. Sounds simple, doesn't it? Yet 'the average board operates on automatic pilot'.[3]

In some respects it's silly to be surprised at the way we manage to skip over this whole facet of 21st-century life. Executives never want regulation or complication to interrupt their business models. They are hostile to rigorous corporate governance and corporate social responsibility because these concepts make them think harder and present problems that they used to ignore (or push onto someone else). But we need different rules and more thoughtful business models for thriving in today's different and more difficult environment. And besides, in a joined-up competitive world there is only so long you can ignore reality before other forces make you change your approach.

The 2005 conviction of WorldCom's chief executive Bernie Ebbers of fraud, was a great day for the champions of better corporate governance. That decision said that ignorance was no excuse and that the buck did stop with someone, even in the labyrinth of a major corporation. If that argument applies in the US it certainly applies in Australia.

We would all be better off if the Australian business community took seriously the idea that good corporate governance can prevent companies making losses or collapsing. And there's a better than even chance that investors will feel more secure saving and investing if they know competent ethical people are spending their capital. Considering those points it's rather sad, but necessary, for the OECD to propose to tighten its principles of corporate governance.[4] These were rules designed to teach Asia and the former Soviet Union lessons in how proper capitalists do things – now the proper capitalists are being sent back to school! This also demonstrates there's a role for government in these matters: they should be acting as catalysts for change by simply talking about these issues. If they won't lead we need to latch onto the corporate insiders who will. 'Transparency is the best guarantee of good outcomes, outcomes we deserve as citizens and which will underpin our growth as an economy.'[5]

We will know we have embedded this mentality and got ourselves a proper corporate sector when we see more:

- staggered board elections (i.e. when talents beats cliques)
- separated chairperson and chief-executive functions (hello, conflict of interest!)
- senior meetings held if the CEO can't be around (if it can't happen without them, it shouldn't happen at all)
- shareholders electing directors on detailed and independently verifiable information on their skills and recent performance
- negligent directors going to jail.

P.S. the idea that the corporation is a structure that can create profits which individuals can reap but where there is no or little individual responsibility when something goes wrong is repulsive to my generation. It's neither clever nor useful, it's just selfish and unethical. We all live on the same planet, so show some respect. If I walk into a shop and break a plate – I pay for it. If you fuck up a company because you are negligent then you are punished.

CORPORATE SLUMS

Jailed tycoons or not, you will know we have failed if we see more debacles like the National Australia Bank trading affair. 'Risk management controls were seen as trip wires to be negotiated rather than presenting any genuine constraint on risk-taking behaviour,' according to the Australian Prudential Regulation Authority (APRA – the body meant to regulate these processes!). To which we should also respond – 'and who's investigating you, APRA?'

Why is it that our corporates are slyly sanctioned to take gross risks with other people's money, or pay $50,000 a year to puppet directors to attend six meetings a year, yet when it comes to investing in useful things – like young people and new ideas – we don't risk a toe nail? Businesses need skilled workers – which they evidently do not have enough of, as even John Howard admits – a lot more than they need to crush unions in the 21st century. So where is the investment on their part to achieve this aim? Where is the might of government to support them in this project?

Business journalism

Australia's immeasurably shonky business journalism cannot be relied upon to provide the scrutiny needed to promote better corporate governance or a wider strategic view of and for Australian corporations, their suppliers and consumers. Sure, there's the *Australian Financial Review* for the junkies, but only one percent of the population reads it. For the rest, our business news is reduced to the flashing of exchange rates and the All Ordinaries at 6.17 p.m. on the nightly news. All Ordinary indeed. When business is reported in Australia it is almost always through the lens of self-interest (how certain stocks are doing, who's manoeuvring to buy out whom) and never public interest. Until it's too late. Then the scandal becomes a colourful, personal news story with a fall guy, stakeouts at mansions and expense accounts laid bare in court. It's drama, not systems analysis.

PLEASE JUST F* OFF . . . IT'S OUR TURN NOW

The fledgling but spirited journalist and shareholder activist Stephen Mayne provided an interesting account of his time as a News Limited business journalist in the 1990s. 'Me and Phillip Morris (the tobacco company) had a great relationship. They must have spent $40,000 all up on me in 10 years.' When I put it to Mayne that business journalism in Australia was either 'absent or shonky' he lamented that 'we used to think it was a great day (when Business Editor at the *Herald Sun*) if we printed one story that was not generated by the Stock Exchange or a press release.'

We can be sure that corporations will continue to get away with what they do because they do not face the same scrutiny as politicians. There is no press gallery for business. The HIH and OneTel collapses were a shock because there was no digging by journalists beforehand. No leaks, no nothing. Companies know they can do as they damn well please.

The corporate constitution

Democracy and its subsequent innovation, fairness and energy are the least we should aim for with corporations. If we want control over our lives we surely have to admit that it can't happen for most people unless we cement decent corporate governance and corporate social responsibility and then aim one step further – embedding a bit of democracy in the corporate sector.

Given the flexibility and dynamism of companies compared to the largely moribund institutions of government, one can only wonder what companies would be able to do to reinvigorate our broader understanding and use of democracy if they had the incentive to try.

When I first saw 'management guru' Charles Handy speak in 1999 it was twee and boring. At a $750 a head (thank God I wasn't paying) for a corporate talk at the Sydney Wesley Mission Centre I sat there thinking – who is worth that money? And in a house of religion? Enough already. Years later his ideas for reforming corporations and driving innovation are both more developed and more radical. It's his campaign for the 'corporate constitution' that captures the imagination.

According to Handy, 'it is a paradox that in our democratic societies it is only the corporations that are resolutely undemocratic.' However, corporations do experience a form of negative democracy where 'people vote with their feet rather than with their ballot papers'.[6] He says that federalism is a concept that can be applied to corporations in a way that allows a good degree of central control but also elements of direct democracy and devolved powers in areas that directly concern particular individual or groups of employees. One presumes these constitutions would be written, open to amendment and appeal by shareholders and would provide the day-to-day framework for board level decision-making. In 2005 after the string of de-mutualisations over recent decades only a handful of employee-owned and charitable or political organisations have such constitutions. That's strange – because I can't imagine too many people my age would choose to keep the current corporate system if given the choice.

Executive and equal pay

You don't need to think we ought to run our Top 100 companies like happy little Bolshevik collectives to see the problems with the way some people are paid in Australia. You just need to believe in natural justice. Part of corporate governance is about having good mission statements and sticking to them. If you can't pay your biggest asset fairly why should we believe anything else you say?

The CEO of the Commonwealth bank earns 307 times the salary of a customer service representative, while ANZ's head of strategy apparently got a $14 million 'mates rates' home loan – a favour not uncommon for senior bankers in this country.[7]

Why on earth would talented ambitious women stay in the Neanderthal economy of Australia? In the US women aged 25–34 earn an average of 112 percent of what men do. In Italy it's between 95 and 100 percent, with most other European countries around the 90 percent mark.[8] In Australia women still earn, on average, about 80 percent of what men do. That's about $200 a week less. Any serious corporate culture would have addressed the issue of equal pay by now. It's not as though you could find a more basic issue that, when dealt with properly, corrects injustice and increases profits by better utilising human capital.

Corporations discriminate on the basis of age as well. It's more than a decade since the then Industrial Relations Commission ruled in favour of implementing equal wages by the turn of the 21st century. We are still waiting. This policy sees people under 21 on wages barely breaching five dollars an hour paid less than their older colleagues to do exactly the same job. The fact that most of the low-paid jobs under this regime are 'unskilled' means that anyone can do them as well as anyone else, so the premise of the legislation is absurd.

Most young people aren't actually affected by junior pay legislation though, because employers know they won't keep talented young people on such low pay rates. How stupid must the law be then? The law inhibits stable employment because people hate the wages and leave as soon as possible; it militates against skill development; and it hands a subsidy to the industries that employ most of the young people affected: supermarkets and fast food.

And we think it's the unemployed rather than corporations that get an easy ride from government? Whatever. Corporations should behave as the rest of us have to.

Corporate Social Responsibility, Social Enterprise and Philanthropy

> Social entrepreneurship – that's where the action is. That's where the real innovators are. That's where you will find the people who will be remembered 50 to 100 years from now.[9]

Corporate Social Responsibility (CSR) is nothing more than the implementation of acceptable standards. It is about society as a whole laying down markers and everyone sticking to them. The markers could relate to the fair treatment of employees, customers, suppliers or other stakeholders not directly involved in a given business (residents next to an airport, for instance).[10]

Non-financial accounting, epitomised by the fad for triple-bottom-line accounting, is the best example of business-minded CSR. Accounting examples are important because advocates of CSR need to get better at measuring the benefits of adhering to CSR principles. Just as we need to prove that being environmentally friendly is good for business we need to prove that being socially responsible is good for business. If the benefits are not measurable then the argument for CSR doesn't exist. Doing CSR in an amateur way to be nice is simply replacing current mediocre business practices with new mediocre ones.

When done well, CSR is a long-term investment strategy. Just as capitalism may not have survived the 20th century without the welfare state, it will struggle without accepting that is must take full account of its environmental and, to a lesser extent, social impact in the 21st century.

As we develop our ability to measure the benefits of CSR there are plenty of other innovations Australian businesses can engage in. Philanthropy, for starters. In the USA about more than $250 billion is given away every year and there are 56,000 charitable foundations.[11] In Australia corporate social responsibility might have an image associated with Red Nose Day and spare change for Ronald McDonald House, but the USA is proof that when a culture chooses a different philanthropic mindset it can be a way of life that transforms the businesses that support it and the lives on individuals who are supported by it. The pattern that acts as the link between all initiatives of this nature is they are win-win situations. The crude aspects of generational conflict are a zero-sum game, but CSR and philanthropy are not. Cirque du Soleil, to point to one example, sends one percent of its gross revenue into social projects – more than $US65 million to date. Its programs have also proven to be great tools for recruitment and staff retention, both because people want to work for companies that care and because it explains promotion and personal development options within the company.[12] If it can work in a structure as fluid as a circus, the message is that Corporate Social Responsibility can work anywhere.

But why just give from the top when you can give up, down and across society. Charitable philanthropy has its uses, but they are outnumbered and out-performed by other species of philanthropy, such as social enterprise. If we in the 21st century are to change the world in the way Carnegie or Rockefeller have done, we will certainly need functioning marketplaces that bring people together to invest in social things.

Social Enterprise and its potential

Can you imagine Australia's wealthiest people giving away more than $200 billion in their lifetimes?[13] That sum is our equivalent of the work of Carnegie and Rockefeller and their legacy institutions – and we will never get there without more sophisticated ways of matching the money with the passion and ideas. There is more money sitting in venture capital funds now that at the height of the Dotcom boom in the late '90s and more of it should be going to social enterprises.

That's certainly not going to happen until 'Social Enterprise' is at least a part of our vocabulary. A definition is called for:

> Social entrepreneurship is the concept of applying the best of entrepreneurial business practices to effect sustainable, positive social change. Just as entrepreneurs define new approaches to business, social entrepreneurs act as agents of social change, identifying opportunities others miss, refining existing social systems, and creating sustainable solutions to improve specific segments of society.[14]

The UK's School for Social Enterprise, until recently headed by former head of the UK Prime Minister's Strategy Unit Geoff Mulgan, former head of Tony Blair's Strategy Unit, and with Cheryl Kernot on the books, is breaking new ground in this field. Elsewhere, former eBay President Jeff Skoll is leading the charge to put the phrase on our lips (he's the third wealthiest person under 40 in the US according to *Forbes*). He's funded a centre for social entrepreneurship at Oxford University no less and pumped $US7.5 million into his Skoll Foundation. We can look forward to global forums, international networks and 'a taxonomy of social entrepreneurship both to set the frame of reference for future research and to identify agendas for new social enterprise start-ups'.[15]

Social Enterprises are, in a sense, what work-for-the-dole schemes should be like – a hard-headed circle of mutual responsibility and action rather than an ideological dead end.

PLEASE JUST F* OFF . . . IT'S OUR TURN NOW

Citibank's shame: a case study of corporate crap

As I type this section I have just received a call at my Redfern digs. It is from Citibank and what I hear at the end of the line is: 'This is a call from Citibank – please hold for an important message from Citibank'. I am now on hold and have been for five minutes waiting for this important message, which is odd given that no one has been nominated as the intended recipient for the call. We'll never know who it was for because the message never comes because no one in the Citibank call centre is available to talk to me because they don't actually care about me like they say. It's now been ten minutes – so what is that all about? A computer now randomly calls my house to deliver me messages from a corporation that I actually hate with a passion.

Here's another Citibank story. In 1998 I took out a student Visa card with Citibank. It all seemed quite nice at the time – them helping me into a credit rating and all. It started to go sour when they started charging me late payment fees of $10 for every 10 days late I was making a repayment – which itself was usually only $30. Which would be annoying, except that I kept getting the statements about two days before the payment was due. By 2002 I had almost forgotten the card existed because they had refused to increase my limit to even $750 and I thought – bugger it – I'll never use it again, and just pay them the minimum each month. Then I stopped getting statements altogether. Before I realised this the late payment fees had pushed me over my credit limit, so I incurred more charges. My card was not renewed at its expiry date. When I rang to ask why I had stopped getting statements they asked me if I wanted to increase my credit limit, and then they realised this wouldn't work because they had cancelled my card. Furious but helpless I spent the next year paying it off. But again Citibank was backdating my statements and sending them out too slowly, so by the time of the final payment I had actually over-paid them $62. They refused to close the account and repay me saying it needed to be left open for six months to see if anyone else charged anything to it – despite the account being shut down more than a year earlier. Five months after that they did allow a $20 charge onto the cancelled card. I finally got my $42 after my parents contacted them (having moved house twice and left the country while the saga continued). I will not be going back.

ING Direct in contrast set up an online account for me in 15 minutes. I've never paid a cent in fees to them, they issue statements on demand and they're polite. There is a lesson in that.

GOOD journalism helps define the character of societies. Its absence leads to societies that are more mediocre in every way.

Eric Beecher

CHAPTER NINE

The Australian mediocracy

Sick and tired of reading the same BORING, predictable drivel day in, day out from a bunch of smug, unimaginative social climbers and liars... Like us do you cringe every time you open the paper, tune into the radio or TV and know exactly what you are going to be told? Had a bellyful of the provincial, self-congratulation, snobbery, cowardice and petulance that passes for debate in this parish pump of a town (Sydney)?[1]

Yes, actually. The sport-obsessed Australian media is a collective yawn. I love sport, I just don't love tedium. However, with the highest concentration of media ownership of all advanced countries, an adversarial model of journalism, plenty of idiotic talkback radio specimens, greedy proprietors and negligent legislators we're stuck with cookie-cutter lowest common denominator media for a while.[2]

The lack of distinct competing views in the Australian mainstream media is, above all other points, a sign of the arrogance of the proprietors (who, regardless of what they or others say, set the political tone of an organisation), and many of the editors and journalists themselves. It's inconceivable that in a world as extremely complex as ours, whose inhabitants have such vastly different experiences, our mainstream media consensus is anything but artificial. Channel Nine is not 'Australian for News', as its advertising campaign goes. They are not put there by divine decree, nor are they elected, no one organisation can be 'Australian for news'.

If we are, as a nation or world, to have any reasonable shot at successfully addressing the challenges before us we need access to the most varied number of opinions and ideas possible. It's essential that we ask why we don't get it, demand improvement and simply circumvent the system until we get it.

It can be different. A new blog is created every second, as are ten blog posts.[3] They are the new New Journalism. Seven of the 25 most powerful people in the British media are under 40.[4] Spread-spectrum technology or even an open spectrum for TV and radio are real and possible. The Open Source software movement is challenging Microsoft's kingdom just as the peer-to-peer networking revolution of music downloads and Creative Commons licensing are redefining the purpose and limits of copyright.[5]

The alternative is our status quo of falling newspaper sales, static TV viewing and democracy weak at home just as it reaches a critical mass globally. We place our trust in local newspapers (not known for their probing journalism) and unmediated material like junk mail.[6]

But then, even if you trusted metropolitan daily newspapers, why would you read them? If you are under 35 and not a criminal, footballer, Olympian or Paris Hilton you're not represented or reflected in them. I bet you can't name a semi-serious columnist under 30. Why? There aren't any. And except for the Adelaide *Advertiser*'s Mia Handshin and *The Australian*'s Emma Tom, I can't think of one from the past decade either. A month-long survey I conducted in April 2004 of *The Australian* and *Sydney Morning Herald* showed that 80 percent of opinion page columns are written by men, a finding one writer on the New Matilda website (www.newmatilda.com.au) echoes vividly: 'The voices of authority that I hear on my radio, on my television, in the meetings that I go to are the voices of men. Unless it's Triple J, or community radio, they're old men.'[7] Even teen movies are reviewed by old hands who've been doing the same gig for decades. Where else but Australia?

I want to be clear that criticising the Australian media doesn't mean that I hate it. Whether at home in Coffs Harbour or online in London, I still read and watch it every day; certainly good journalism and great laughs can be enjoyed. But a top-shelf media industry doesn't need to be reminded of those good points constantly. It does need to be reminded of its failings, and the mature response is to recognise that this process is not a personal insult. Criticism should lead to improvement, not paralysis.

Journalism doesn't have to be like this

One News Limited journalist told me she is instructed when seeking case studies and vox pops: 'now, remember, no Asians, just nice white Aussie kids ...' Another claimed that a (Sydney) *Sunday Telegraph* photographer answered her question about why so many blonde white women appeared in the paper with: 'It's about presenting eastern suburbs people and lifestyles to Western suburbs people.' Then there's an ABC radio recruit being told to imagine he was talking to his neighbours over the fence in Epping, a less-than-dynamic Sydney suburb. Worried? All that is saintly compared to *Daily Telegraph* management antics – according to a former employee, the maverick Stephen Mayne:

> Muslims were regularly referred to as 'towelheads' by Col Allan [then editor] ... One copy kid was screamed at and told he'd never get a cadetship when he brought the wrong utensil for Col to eat his lunch with. During one Christmas drinks, it was suggested that respected

columnist Sandra Lee be invited to join 'the boys' in Col's office, to which he replied: 'Nahh, no fat chicks allowed.'[8]

Journalists from other newspapers described to me how executives would send them in taxis to pay off potential defamation litigants with envelopes of cash: 'It was the norm'. Jane Robinson, a former producer and researcher for *Four Corners*, the *7.30 Report* and *Stateline*, was scathing of the standards and style of Australian journalism when she spoke to me: 'Journalism is not about analysing in Australia. It's a game show about proving the politician wrong. It's all adversarial and not analytical.' Veteran media analyst Julianne Schultz is even less sympathetic. She finds the press galleries guilty of 'cartoon journalism that fills in the blanks of a script which has been substantially written'.[9] But for those who like to think Australian has passed on from a 'golden age' of journalism, they can stop now. Even the great Phillip Knightley, now 76 and a Member of the Order of Australia admits he made up a story about a non-existent sexual pervert when working for Sydney's *Truth* (hmm) newspaper in the 1950s.[10]

The slow death of free-to-air television

Euthanasia is the best description of this process – one of choice, not circumstance. Australian free-to-air television companies choose to live in a time warp, and the government chooses to support that corporate lifestyle. If the government were to ban new newspapers or spaces for public discussion there would be an outcry.[11] Yet when the government preserves a dinosaur oligopoly in free-to-air TV it achieves the same thing. We live with a 'benign paternalism' that the UK and US gave up years ago.[12] Consequently younger people are switching off and taking other, more interactive choices. In contrast the interactive television options that are freely available in US and European television meet the desires of a new generation to control, personalise and participate in their media experience.[13]

Even those that remain as free-to-air viewers are starting to ignore the ads that fund the business model.[14] 'Most companies admit that television advertising isn't persuading young people to buy their products'.[15] But with up to 16 minutes of ads per hour you can have quite cheap rates and still be operating a cash cow, so there's no incentive to improve either the advertising or the programming.

For 27-year-old Melburnian Emily Mierisch, the old TV news jingle 'I know everything I need to know because Brian told me, Brian told me so,' is the epitome of what's wrong with Australian media.[16] It's the inane and close-minded production and consumption that grates with her. Indeed, it defies intellectual credibility that any person could be the best person for a particular job for more than 40 years in a row – but somehow that's what Channel Nine thought of Brian Henderson (and Channel Nine rehiring Bert Newton? Lame, Lame, Lame). In other news today: no news or current affairs programme makes it into Top 50 watched by 14–24-year-olds.

Lack of interest in news is not the problem. According to a leading member of the team behind Vibewire Youth Services (**www.vibewire.net**), Simon Moss:

> 'The media hasn't grappled at all with how young people engage with information. They struggle to understand how the world works. For example, I was quite upset when they axed Fly TV – Fly made really good moves into how media is likely to be consumed in the next 10 years.' He went on to ask: 'Hamish and Andy (the young comedy duo) got given two shows on Channel Seven in 2004 – how can you prove anything in two weeks?'

Vibewire Youth Services has conducted the most comprehensive series of surveys of youth attitudes to media in 21st century Australia – with more than 700 respondents – and its findings are clear. News about celebrities rates well behind global issues, politics, education, relationships and friends.[17]

The free-to-air monoliths will only cease to be lame and nauseating if a more competitive and sophisticated television market is developed. A fourth commercial network, a second or third ABC channel and a proper Digital TV system are the baseline for this cultural change. UK's More4, the digital Channel 'love child of Channel 4', defines what I mean by this claim. It is, in its own words, 'one finger on the pulse and another defiantly raised to convention. (Reclaiming) territory for free-thinking, open-minded grown-ups who want to be challenged as well as entertained.'[18]

Not exactly what you find on 'your' ABC these days.

The ABC: domain of the white over-forties

The ABC is now the domain of the white over-forties. It's axing innovations like the youth-oriented digital service Fly TV is symbolic of both the screwing up of digital TV policy and the screwing over of young people. ABC has two substantive channels, the BBC Eight. Australia has no real digital TV, the UK has 28 stations. The Australian TV community can't spell 'interactive' while the UK has 190 options and several hundred 'pay TV' channels.[19] The main public argument for digital TV in Australia seems to be better picture quality, which is like arguing for cars over horses because they smell less. Macquarie Bank bought the digital services arm of the BBC, called BBC Broadcast, in July 2005 – it's pretty sad they have nothing similar to invest in at home.[20]

The contrast between the dynamism of the BBC and the aimless ABC is stark. The BBC has even been accused of having 'an obsession with 25–34s'.[21] Not so at the ABC – 'while ABC TV's share of viewers 55 and over and children has increased since 1990, its share of viewers 18–39 has declined by 13 percent'.[22] Their supporters' base think of themselves as 'progressive' but are more 'comfortable in the role of conservatives, championing a status quo that serves their needs very well'.[23] Friends of the ABC will bemoan the decline of radio drama before tackling a more ambitious and positive agenda that includes phrases like 'digital', 'young people' and 'innovation'.[24] It is surprising that people who care about the ABC aren't willing to go out on more of a limb for it. Innovation in content and delivery is not just more interesting, but the bedrock of quality journalism and entertainment. Yet the supporters of the ABC just want the same old same old, to turn the clock back to some golden age. Properly invested in, there is a far greater chance of new material being profitable in both a financial and cultural sense than something which is tired and old.

The ABC need not ditch the tired and old though if only it took up the cause of multi-channeling more seriously. It could have both old and new if there was a second or even third free-to-air channel. All of their channels should go digital, in addition to any expansion of the number. Labor called for a 'Triple Jay of Television' in its 2004 election campaign, but the name doesn't matter. The ABC itself agrees it could have two proper digital channels for $35 million a year and it's vital that it pursues this regardless of the government funding environment and achieves what BBC Three has done in Britain: 'constantly pushing the terrestrial BBC's envelope.'[25]

Once upon a time it was: 'someone was brave enough to take a punt on . . . the *This Day Tonight* boys when they were callow youths.'[26] Four of the people who have dominated public broadcasting in Australia for 30 years were from the same cadet group (George Negus, Paul Lyneham, Mike Carlton and Kerry O'Brien). That's not luck – that's a betrayal of all the talented potential journalists since the 1970s who have not been given the opportunities they deserve. That lot got to write their 'first rough draft of history' in their twenties – and they are still broadcasting it in our faces more than three decades later.[27] When will we get to write ours?

'There has to be an inner circle, but it has to be perpetually capable of being gatecrashed by the talented and bold.'[28] So says the BBC genial former political editor Andrew Marr and I hope the ABC starts listening to that message now because major transformation is needed to achieve that culture:

> THE agenda at the ABC is set by a group of intelligent people, but they are all over 45, have worked together for years, have an agreed agenda, and if you're not from that background you can't get your views across. I worked for five EPs (Executive Producers) at Four Corners – they had all worked together for decades, they were all married or had affairs or other significant relationships with each other . . . If you're weren't from there, if you didn't fit in, you couldn't go anywhere. You had to leave. There is absolutely no sense of regeneration.
>
> *ABC TV producer, female*

ABC Radio is a slightly brighter place to be if you're in public broadcasting or indeed an ordinary occasional listener. For at ABC radio you can tune into the stalwart JJJ or hear young voices on the flagship current affairs programs like AM. Around the turn of the millennium I have been led to believe there was even a minor fracas over the claim that *too many* young people were being promoted to good and powerful journalist postings. Many of the beneficiaries were in their twenties at the time and continue to acquit themselves well: Jonathan Harley (India), Geoff McDonald (Asia), Sally Sara (Africa), Lisa Miller (Washington) and now Raphael Epstein in London.

Radio

The withholding of FM radio licences when there are groups crying out for them is a genuine Aussie tragedy. There are more than 1000 private radio stations in Turkey, for God's sake![29] The UK just announced plans to allow another 100 new digital radio stations – on top of the 210 already operating.[30] Why are there such strict controls on Australia's radio bandwidth? It's not like we are going to run out and jeopardise essential emergency communication channels. The technology even exists to reuse bandwidth these days. So let's start thinking along the lines of the early days of radio in the US. This was a golden era of democracy in communication as radio amateurs communicated with each other in a spirit of idealism and fun, concepts far removed from the automated playlists of the 'classic hits from the '60s, '70s and '80s'.[31]

Must the biggest news in radio really permanently revolve around Alan Jones and John Laws and their reactionary audiences? 'Every male radio presenter in Australia has the same voice and the same fake blokey-jokey style,' Emily Mierisch rightly complains. Says Darren Armstrong: 'I know what the secret sound is – a promotional gambit by a radio station without an original idea, played on excessively high rotation.'[32]

How can we have lost the spirit and retracted the autonomy that allowed Triple J to transform the lives of regional youth in the 1980s and '90s? Margaret Throsby's twenty-something daughter recently recounted for *The Australian* how she landed a job programming the in-flight music selection for seven small airlines while she was still a teenager. She put Velvet Underground on Air Namibia. Can we have more of that risk-taking in Australia please?

Broadband

It should be the new public utility of the 21st century. On tap like water and free, or virtually free, at the point of use. It is a disgrace that the federal government has not used libraries and empty shops in regional towns and filled them with cheap computers and Internet access. You could purchase, accommodate and maintain between 50–100,000 desktop PCs with broadband access for less than the estimated cost of Australia's involvement in stage one of the war

PLEASE JUST F* OFF . . . IT'S OUR TURN NOW

> ## Things we hate about the Australian media
>
> 1 *60-year-old newsreaders.*
>   Just shoot them. Then bring in some of Jessica Rowe types (of either sex that is).
>
> 2 *Cash-for-trash 'journalism'.*
>   a.k.a. *A Current Affair* and *Today Tonight*. You know you have lost your moral compass when you watch that shit.
>
> 3 *Multichannelling? What's that?*
>   Get on the Internet and find out – it's called the very-well-recognised future.
>
> 4 *Our Libel Laws.*
>   If you can demonstrate that an opinion is merely 'reasonable', then you should be allowed to express it. We sweep ideas under the carpet at the threat of lawsuits – it makes our public discourse bland and simply encourages the black art of self-censorship.
>
> 5 *The group think of the Canberra Press Gallery.*
>   The Gallery is a club, and like all clubs acts out of self-interest. Coupled with taxpayer funded political PR spoon-feeding the Gallery is getting lazy. How about visiting a Senate Committee or meeting real people and then writing about them?

in Iraq in 2003.[33] So why hasn't it happened? Where is our social enterprise and government imagination? While the rest of the world figures out how to move past the platform of the world wide web we remain stuck trying to make effective use of it. In Australia the standard broadband is 256k – people in the developed world smirk when told that. The bare minimum should be 512k – and many places are four to 40 times faster than that. The lamentable lack of Australian broadband choice is an embarrassment to us all.

Innovations the Australian media ought to try

1 *Tabloid transformation.*
    The Times, The Independent and *The Guardian* did it and so can Australian broadsheets. It's time for compacts with impact. Small-size papers without the small-minded journalism.

2 *Readers' panels.*
    The *Chicago Tribune* boasts a 300-strong set of readers who provide daily critiques and vetoes on matters from headlines to layout.

3 *Citizen reporters* – a la **OhMyNews.com**.

4 *Columnists under 35.*

5 *Free web archives* – *Guardian Unlimited* gets up to a million unique visitors a day and their archive is the main draw card.

Web reporting

While News Limited produces terrible news websites to save money and Fairfax bizarrely attempts to implement user pays to its websites as though they are porn services, Len Downie, editor of the *Washington Post*, is the one who is actually on the mark. He is campaigning to reduce the profitability of newspapers. Downie says that newspaper owners should settle for less profit – and given that the profit margins for newspapers are often three or four times that of other leading companies like supermarkets, there's little argument against it.[34] To allow shareholder greed to triumph over democracy would be a horrible legacy for our grandchildren. They deserve better than Paris Hilton as headline news.

More money should be spent on projects like web platforms and decent investigative journalism, and to hit the point precisely – Australian media companies *can* spend more money. But even if they choose not to spend more money there are still other ways to do journalism differently.

You may not have heard of **OhMyNews.com** – but you will. South Korea's new premier news service is changing the shape of news media markets in ways that may last for decades to come. It's the journalistic equivalent of Open Source software. OhMyNews's 35 staff reporters are propped up by 35,000 'citizen reporters' – ordinary Joe Blow's and aspiring journalists who have been churning out the scoops in exchange for pocket money (about $25) since February 2000. Readers leave tips for good stories (80 percent of which are written by the citizen reporters, and 40 percent of whom are aged 20–29) and the customer base is overwhelmingly young.[35] Run by a reformed student radical, Oh Yeon-Ho, his motto 'Every citizen is a reporter' is catching on fast in a country where almost everyone has a camera phone and the broadband penetration is the highest on the planet.[36] The website alone gets 20 million page views per day.[37]

This media machine has been able to attract advertising revenue and also dabbles in web-casting, web radio, text-casting, and a weekly print version. So why in a country such as Australia, renowned as a site of fast adoption of new technologies, have we seen nothing like it? According to the *Far Eastern Economic Review* it's 'a medium that's here to stay', yet in our allegedly slick, entrepreneurial economy we've seen no movement beyond the anonymous bitching of *Crikey*. Margo Kingston's *Web Diary* on **smh.com.au** is the only thing that comes close to **OhMyNews.com** and its audience appeal is too narrow to ever scale the same heights.

Blogs

They are tedious, mostly crap and many of the popular ones are by dodgy journalists who are loose with the facts (hello, Matt Drudge are you reading this?). Regardless, they are balancing the power between audiences and the media elite and they deserve all the increasing attention they are getting. In response to blogs we are now seeing Reader's Editors pages, readers panels whose members actively and daily contribute to editorial decisions, and millions of new sources for polemical content. *The Australian* was reasonably on the ball in publishing bloggers before they hit the mainstream – but they are alone in that achievement. Others will have to join them though. Like my generation, blogs are inclusive and encourage accountability, and that means they will be around as long as we are (well, those of us who don't leave the country, at least).

If forced to sum up Australian media as we leap into the 21st century we must confront many sad realities. Wherever you look the same three structural flaws keep appearing. It's not young enough, it's not diverse enough and it's not innovative enough. As a package that's an unbeatable collection of arguments for telling Baby Boomers the party's over. Leading countries are in a state of media reform and upheaval. Blogs, broadband, digital TV switchovers, mass expansion of radio options, compact newspapers, innovative public broadcasting and young journalists. In Australia, we have the fledgling *Crikey*, the effects of Telstra's near monopoly on our broadband market, a ritual killing of digital TV, talkback tragedy, threatened further concentration of media ownership, a deadbeat public broadcaster, broadsheets getting dumb instead of compact and a set of political and social commentators who will still be sent pay cheques in their graves because no one noticed the difference. You couldn't write a more comical script – but why would you? No one would hire you to bring it to life anyway.

IN Australia there really isn't a lot to do. There aren't a lot of opportunities.
Radha Mitchell, actor[1]

CHAPTER TEN

Generation eXpat

We've got these skilled people. We have to give them a good reason to stay ... We have to recognise that we are in a competitive global marketplace for skills, and we have to ensure we can compete. There are a number of factors operating here ... perhaps the most important are world class research facilities and a culture of innovation that rewards these heroes.

That was Richard Alston talking to The Sydney Institute in 2000. We can take his relocation to London to join the rest of Generation eXpat as an indication that he didn't fulfil his vision. We can also look to the empirical evidence. Forty-four percent of business owners report an acute shortage of skilled workers in 2005, compared with 30 percent in 2004 (behind only New Zealand and Russia in expressing such concerns).[2] And, of course, roughly half of my Australian friends have left and now live in the same tube zone as me in London.

Why did I leave? The suffocation. The dread of knowing that in early 21st century Australia you get on by keeping in line. Every member of Generation eXpat has their own particular tipping point. I felt I could bash my head against a brick wall or get on with my life

PLEASE JUST F* OFF . . . IT'S OUR TURN NOW

somewhere else and hope that a niche would exist for me one day in the country that I love. The crunch was probably campaigning in the 2001 Federal Election. Living off a salary of $20,000, I would fly monthly to Coollangatta and campaign door-to-door for the brilliant 28-year-old Labor candidate Jenny McAllister. The refugee issue was tough, but what really broke my heart was opening a centrally produced pack to find an insert labelled *Labor's Cancer Plan*. Is that what the Labor party has been reduced to? Who supports cancer? I knew then that I had to leave.

More than a million of my fellow Australians have made the same choice. It's not a new cultural cringe; Generation eXpat is too diverse and too many want to return to Australia for us to get stuck with the cultural cringe label. It's human capital flight and it's driven by economics, lack of opportunity and inertia in public life. We love Australian but not the 'Southern Hemisphere Ceiling', or the tolerance of mediocrity that now comes with it.

We owe it to ourselves as a nation to ask why we allow the potential of these people to be diverted or wasted. Some of it is inevitable – the consequence of a being a small country, with small markets compared to global giants like China and the established middleweights like the UK. As Bernard Salt thundered at me down a phone line from the other side of the world: 'Opportunities in Australia are piddling . . . if you are dynamic there [are] simply more opportunities overseas than here in the colonies and that's one of the best elements of globalisation.' But there is a point where all this ceases to be inevitable and becomes national Hari Kari. It's a process where so much talent is sucked away that eventually all you are left with, in the words of Salt, are 'the old, the complacent and the ugly'.

'It's exactly the same as the best being sucked out of regional Australia to the cities,' he says, and Adelaide is the perfect example of this. One 29-year-old interview subject was in raptures about Adelaide. 'Don't you notice how all the best people are from Adelaide.

They are always smart and funny and cultured. I've never met a bad one,' she crowed. And then I asked how often she visits Adelaide. 'Oh, I don't,' was the reply. That's because most of the good young people have left and she meets them in the places they have fled to.

> The cosmopolitan elite of Adelaide have the most wonderful lifestyle imaginable. They have it all but there's no depth and there's nothing for the next generation. It is a flawed Eden that involves a generational fault line. Yes you as a Boomer can have this wonderful life but the punishment is your children have to live in another state or country.[3]

Do we really want to see this repeated across the country – the Adelaide-isation of Australia?

Depth is a key word in this debate. World cities have a certain depth that I don't notice in Sydney or Melbourne. This occurred to me, on a trip back to Australia in October 2005, as I contemplated just how many beautiful people there are in both cities. But something was missing. Style. The people I was gawping at had an amazing appearance, but at the end of the day it was shallow. Beyond the great tans and toned limbs was a decisive lack of thought about what their dress sense said to the world. It was different to other, colder parts of the world, but in a lazy rather than innovative way. Wearing thongs to a cocktail evening isn't stylish no matter how hot the weather is.

I spoke to several people in the fashion industry as a 'sanity check' on my thoughts. Their views on this identi-kit behaviour and what it means for them were forthright, if nothing else:

> MY problem is my definition of success. I don't think that success equals money – I think it's about being the best 'you' can be. If I wanted to make money or get recognition here I would design slutty little dresses for Sydney princesses, take coke with the right people and go to their parties. But I don't

want that to be my route to success, so I have to leave or go it about the hard way.

Anonymous, former Australian Fashion Week award winner

That interview subject is far from alone. Indeed, the best thing I can do to explain Generation eXpat is to let it speak for itself. Direct to you this is what they told me, told the Senate and told newspapers about the country they used to call home.

THE 'lucky country' is a myth. I'm 29, on £80,000 as a financial controller in London . . . if the Australian public and politicians saw just how many of its youth live here and in Europe, permanently, they'd be worried.

Mike in Camden Town, London UK

WORKING in the public sector you have to wait for someone to die or have a baby to get a chance for the job you want, which you then only get on a temporary basis. There is no certainty and no opportunity. And that's why I'm in London – I left to go to a place where there are far more opportunities for me.

Emily Mierisch, 27, London

I got to the point where someone was going to have to retire or die before I moved up to the next level. I left.

Anonymous, 26, Sydney

I left in 2002. I just had the feeling that I was 'too' everything. I was too different. Too ethnic. Too outrageous. Too ambitious. I just couldn't do it any longer. In London being different is why people value you. In Australia it is used to stifle you.

Female, 32, interviewed in Wales

EVERY day I talk to another thirty-something Australian

who wishes they'd done a Kylie and gone or stayed abroad when they had the chance. Here, you should be so lucky as to have a three-year contract as a bottom feeder in an arts faculty . . . There, you'd stand a chance of already being an associate professor, senior political adviser, published author or other established opinion former.

Natasha Cica, Melbourne[4]

For others leaving is simply about 'putting the icing on the cake', or using success in a global market as the way to jump some rungs in the Australian career ladder.

LONDON puts us in a market where we (partner) can work in new ways. Before we left Sydney we were thinking two years. Now we are thinking between two to five.

Rannia Wannous, 28, London

I had done everything that Australia had to offer me. I worked at the highest levels of government and the highest level of media. The logical thing was to take the next step into a world market. Australia prepared me very well for that.

Anonymous

AT the moment there is nowhere for me to go in Australia. It was too easy back home. I needed to be pushed. At the risk of sounding like someone on a journey of self-discovery I needed to be challenged because Australia was making me a bit complacent.

Jo Fox, 31, London

WE use these skills to go back to Australia to deal ourselves back in at a higher level. You set yourself apart from having competed and succeeded in a global marketplace. A global market cuts you down to size. You can get too

> big for Australia but you can't get too big for London or New York.
>
> *Anonymous*

> THERE are far more highly developed structures in Europe. You are forced to respond to so many more influences. The management culture is so much more sophisticated. A lot more is expected of you in the UK. I never found my place in Australia.
>
> *Jane Robinson, London*

If I needed any confirmation of these anecdotes it came in a five-week window through January and February 2005. In that period seven (yes, seven) of my friends of former colleagues joined me to live in London, two booked tickets for trips to investigate permanent relocation, one took 12 months unpaid leave in anticipation of moving, and a final person asked me to help with a high skilled visa application. All to one city, in one foreign country. Either I'm really hot and have 1400 friends and therefore these numbers are insignificant (the answers are no, no and no) or there's some structural problem in Australia that is encouraging them to leave.

The Senate analysed the needs of overseas Australians in 2003. The 600 submissions, with extracts below, are a lot more interesting and up to date than anything Germaine Greer, Clive James or Richard Neville has to say on the subject.[5]

> I moved to England in March 1999. I am a television script writer. Before I left Australia, I worked for *Home and Away* and *Water Rats*. When I was unfairly demoted, I decided to try my luck in the UK. Since I arrived I've had a successful career as both a script editor and a script writer. I found in the UK television industry, people are employed on merit. Talented people get promoted. In Australia, the television industry is ageist. As a 22-year-old woman, it was impossible to get

GENERATION EXPAT

work heading a script department. However, in the UK it took only four months for me to get a job as a sole script editor on *Emmerdale*, UK's third top rating drama . . . This year I'll earn around 65,000 pounds . . . One friend was recently sacked from Channel Seven because her boss 'felt like a change'. She was given no warning. Another friend was told not to wear trainers to work. This kind of thing would never happen in the UK television industry . . . It seems to me you have to be over 35 for anyone in the Australian TV industry to take you seriously, or a bloke.

Holly Lyons, East Sussex, UK

THE opportunities we have (in the UK) are endless. Work wise, the money is so much better than home. You can even organise a job from Australia . . . I will not leave here until I have enough money to go home and put a deposit on a house.

Emma Oliver, London

THE predominant driving factor for my wife and myself (to leave Australia) is the lack of social and economic appreciation for our skills. We both have PhDs in Engineering and Science fields . . . there is definitely a cost to losing the higher education skills overseas.

Steve de Hennin, Ottawa, Canada

I moved to the US in October 2000 after being offered a position by an Australian winery to work for their US partner selling Aussie wine in the US. The job had no down side my salary went from $AU45,000 TO $US95,000 and my tax halved.

Sam Holmes, North Carolina

PLEASE JUST F* OFF . . . IT'S OUR TURN NOW

I live in Dubai. I am the regional manager for a multi-national American company . . . (on returning to Australia) I decided to visit several recruitment agencies, and I was very disappointed to see the lack of opportunities available. I received messages that I was too over-qualified . . . This is the attitude that I feared from a third-world country, not Australia . . . I would come back in three seconds if Australia can wake up and see the light.

Kerry Koutsikos, Dubai

THE smarter Australians are fleeing the country in search of better employment opportunities that they will never receive back home and challenges in their career. We are afforded opportunities that would take a lifetime to receive in Australia due to the prevalent 'old boys network'. God forbid a woman would speak her mind. In America (namely New York) you are encouraged to be your best, constantly challenge your abilities and train others in order to move upward. This is quite the opposite to what I experienced in Australia in the banking sector. The men felt threatened, I experienced sexual harassment . . .

Heidi Rybak, New York

I would prefer to live in Australia but I am an academic and the job prospects and working conditions in Australia were very poor, so I left. This was the factor driving me to live overseas, and it is what will prevent me from returning.

Dr Ruth Abbey, Canterbury, UK

WHEN we are certain that conditions are equally beneficial in Australia, we will be there. I need the employers of Australia to recognise the work experience gained in very challenging environments and senior roles in the UK.

Anna Boltong, London, UK

Flyers, damn frequent flyers and statistics

According to the Australian Bureau of Statistics:

> For the year ended 31 December 2004 net overseas migration was 109,700 persons. During the last two years permanent arrivals and departures have recorded strong growth. Compared with five years ago the annual number of departures are up 41.1 percent.[10]

Some 858,886 Australians declared themselves as living overseas on a permanent basis in 2001 – 4.3 percent of the population. 264,955 additional citizens are living overseas on a short-term basis.[11] That's at least 1.1 million people, or five percent of the population, but the real and current figures are much higher. Australian Bureau of Statistics figures show that permanent or long-term departures of Australian citizens in 2003 (193,525) were approximately 40 percent higher than in 2001 (139,466). In 1993 the figure was just 93,351.[12]

Would we accept an unemployment rate of 10 percent instead of five percent? Hell no – but that is what we put up with when emigration is taken into account.

The Department of Education, Science and Training (DEST) counters that record numbers of people are migrating to OECD countries and that Australia is just part of a 'brain circulation'. Some brave people admit the 'Australian diaspora' but claim that 'on balance' we have had a 'brain gain' of 156,000 skilled workers in the five years to 2001.[13]

I can't dispute the DEST figures but good people are fleeing – and if you are aged 20–40 or have children of that age you know at least one. Even if these people are being replaced, the fact that we give them few reasons to stay is not a good enough public policy response. DEST does admit that 'a high proportion of expatriates are from high skilled occupation areas'.[14] But, in fact, it's a bit more serious than that. The number of employee residents departing Australia has increased by 40 percent since the election of the Howard Government – to

PLEASE JUST F* OFF . . . IT'S OUR TURN NOW

Does Australia have world cities?

Reading the morning papers in the aftermath of the 2005 London bombings, I was struck by the faces of London. 'Like the phone directory of the United Nations . . . their faces . . . could be a photo album from a company committed to diversity.'[6] I see it every morning in the masses as they dart across the concourse at Liverpool Street station; I saw it the afternoon of the bombings as I trudged home in the rain with millions of others. Thirty-two of the 39 photos of victims that stared at us that next morning were under 35. They came from every continent, and in seeing that I realised what a real 'world city' is. It's not easy; it's not white; it's not old. It's crazy and colourful and out of control in a way I don't recognise in Australia.

We have the best fresh and café food in the world but more and more research exists mocking the myth of the fabulous Australian world city – the fifth column after New York, London, Tokyo and Paris. Whether judged by cultural concentration, air travel, NGO activity or finance and global firm headquarters, Sydney and Melbourne don't rate as world cities. Sydney ranks only 30th in terms of air passenger travel (behind London, Frankfurt, Paris, New York and even Cairo), representing a drop of 14 places since 1977.[7] NGO rankings remind us that even places such as Nairobi, Brussels and Bangkok get a big share of global action we miss out on.

The best we can say is that Sydney, Melbourne, Brisbane are 'middle ranked' global cities.[8] The Australian Capital City Report from 1999 shows Sydney accelerating its lead over Melbourne in services to business, finance and property and media and publishing, but the bigger point is that the rest of the world is also accelerating its lead over us. It takes no great leap of the imagination to put Sao Paulo, Rio De Janeiro or Johannesburg on the same footing as Sydney. But it's a real challenge for white chauvinists to think that a Portuguese-speaking city might be more interesting. It is easier to believe that hosting the Olympics was the

> last jewel in Sydney's world city crown, when in fact genuine success is measured over the long haul. Yet we don't have a long term blueprint because we are too busy looking in the mirror admiring ourselves. Primed for this self-indulgence by tourist boards, development agencies, and the society page editors we flatter ourselves into believing our capital cities are 'world cities' – that a good café latte makes us cosmopolitan. Unfortunately, 90 percent of Australia is banal surburbia and 10 percent of our young people are leaving Australia every year for the lure of real urbanity. What are we doing about it?
>
> Our self-satisfied attitudes are part of the problem but unfortunately not the sum of it. In the field of world cities geography really does count against us, making laziness about our future prospects a foolish approach. According to Taylor and Deruder, world cities exhibit extremely cliquish tendencies towards each other and there is a strong regional dimension to their status.[9] The conclusion is that we do not have a world city and we are not going to get one anytime soon with the current lack of serious thought and effort.

around 100,000 a year.[15] Using the example of the education sector, of those who are leaving in their twenties, 78 percent held postgraduate qualifications and 97 percent were employed as professionals before they left Australia.[16]

But it's not adequate to blame Generation eXpat on generous people answering ads to fill skill shortages in England, or high flyers working for multinationals, which is the OECD's analysis. Nor can we assume that migrants are moving back to their families. 'Better employment opportunities' was the reason for 42.6 percent of Australians leaving the country, a fact the Business Council of Australia knows and fears all too well.[17]

If you think we're all off chasing money, you're wrong. My income in Australia bought me a better lifestyle that it does in London. What money doesn't buy is the Management Development

Programme my UK employers signed me up to. It doesn't buy the five days training leave I get every year, the support to do community volunteering on work time, or the choice to pick my hours and work from home when I need to. It doesn't buy a system based on merit and competition. And it doesn't buy the chance to work in an environment where your peers write the best newspaper columns, advise the best politicians, make the best deals in the financial markets and open exhibitions at the best galleries.

Emigration is the simple side of the brain drain/brain gain flow. Imagine the disaster imposed upon poor and tiny island nations losing more than half of their graduates to a bigger country. That's the flip side of our emigration problem. We suck skills and talent from the countries that can least afford to lose those things, in order to replace our own skills losses. According to the World Bank, it is so bad that more than 75 percent of graduates from Tonga and Western Samoa are jumping ship to Australia and New Zealand.[18] Such wild trends of immigration or emigration are irresponsible in the extreme and completely unnecessary – the consequence of a lack of a national blueprint and a culture that is dynamic and exciting and responsible to our citizens and neighbours.

Anyone who is serious about the future of quality public debate and institutions in this country has an obligation to engage with the paucity of both in Australia, and with the people who are so sick of it that they simply leave. Thirty-five years ago there was a similar reassessment that created changes on a scale comparable to those that are needed now. Today we must create specific policies to lure talented young people back. The 2005 increase in the income tax rate thresholds was a good start, but it is not enough.

And it is increasingly apparent that now is the time to figure out exactly what 'enough' is.

CHAPTER ELEVEN

Beige-town politics

'I've never really given a slutty fuck about politics.' Coming from Kerry, a 25-year-old from Perth who spends her life working with homeless people, that statement tells us traditional institutions are failing us.

People are more interested in political issues than ever, but the standard outlets for those feelings are unable to open up and change to accommodate this interest and the way it is most often expressed. Not only are they not changing they are going backwards. In the brutal words of the Labor maverick Rodney Cavalier 'within one generation Bob Hawke has become Steve Hutchins.'[1] And a generation later John Howard and Kim Beazley are still John Howard and Kim Beazley. Compare politics to another sector and notice the lack of equilibrium. Surely it's irony of the highest order that while we have almost unlimited consumer choice we believe we no longer have political choices.

The reasons for disengagement from mainstream politics have nothing to do with the lack of sms voting. We are trying to use systems designed in the early 20th century for people living in the 21st. I don't use an icebox because it wouldn't meet my needs, and many people ask why they should spend a lot of time worrying about who is in parliament when few of its members address their concerns or are willing to respect their confidence and intelligence. It's not rocket science.

The language and framework of politics – concepts like 'left' and 'right' – are increasingly removed from the everyday complexity of most people's lives. Soon enough we will reach a critical mass of faithlessness that undermines the whole edifice. Even when people are moved to political acts many are so alienated from the word 'politics' they simply don't recognise these acts as political.[2] Donating money to an overseas aid organisation is not classed as a 'political' act, for instance, yet it is utterly entangled in politics – from your choice of whether to give to a religious or secular group, to the fact you are giving at all when governments have a greater capacity to give on your behalf. Rather, acts like this are considered as only a 'worthy thing to do', removed from the world of parliaments and council chambers.

Ignoring institutional politics is stupid. It affects every part of your life – at work, how you get to and from work, your ability to fund your lifestyle, the way in which you are perceived by the law and in the community. It doesn't just shape you – you can use political skills and institutions to shape your lives and your communities. Mark Latham's retrospective and bitter advice to young people to stay away from organised politics doesn't stack up. I am reminded of Winston Churchill's view that democracy is the worst system, except for all the others. Very few people want to follow in the footsteps of Natasha Stott Despoja and be a young MP – and cheers to that – but politics does have a role in all our lives, even if it's just as background noise.

What's missing, though, is the sense that politics is about lived experiences – not theories, ideologies and two-party parliamentary jousting. We run Australian politics like our free-to-air television – pumping out the bland and unsophisticated – and look what's happening to the audiences for both. Today we live in a world of niche audiences and markets, and people who live lives of multiple identities. If you want a strong relationship with individuals these days, whether its politics or media, you have to give them the respect that comes with acknowledging their identities. You have to invest that respect in people over a long time. If you don't, it is like 'trying to make microchips using a steam engine'.[3]

What passes as political rhetoric today is so beige, so one size fits all, that it is embarrassing to civilised people. You are judged on which shade of beige you are in a spectrum of static political ideas, not on the quality of your thinking, your potential or your track record. That these positions come from the mouths of a shallow, incestuous gene pool makes it worse. How many times have you heard a no-name MP or junior minister or party leader say outside the doors of parliament a sentence beginning with 'People tell me . . .' or 'What the Australian people want . . .' followed by whatever unoriginal thing they already and always believed.

Or perhaps you just don't even listen anymore. You've probably noticed how instead of trying to identify actual innovative solutions to tangible problems, Aussie politicians stretch their brains trying to find ways to market the problem. We don't need a more nicely worded or prettily presented problem.

Good products, services and answers don't need much marketing – their value is self-evident. Their value does not need to be emphasised with an advertising carpet bomb, as we saw in 2004 with the $123 million deluge of government commercials in the lead up to the election.

Parliament

The same old men in ugly suits asking the same old questions. That covers much of what happens in our parliament.

The long-standing practice of asking Dorothy Dixers – pre-arranged questions from backbenchers, usually written by the answering minister's office – is symbolic of the state of our democracy. No serious institution would permit them. Imagine a staff meeting with prearranged questions which you ask the guy who works in the cubicle next to you. What a joke. Is Australia a better place because of any Dorothy Dixer question? So stop asking them. If you're an MP or Senator who agrees with me – just refuse to ask them, it's really simple. There's a 95 percent chance you're not a complete moron if you got pre-selected and elected, so do something with that brain.

Look at other aspects of our Parliaments to witness further dysfunction. The working hours are horrendously unsocial, political staffers have pernicious control over their bosses and affairs of state, and increasingly staffers are the bosses. Some of our state parliaments sit for as little as ten weeks a year. And let it be noted that there is almost always fewer than five people in either chamber at a given time. Absence is not the disease though – it is the symptom.

An MP's presence in either house is irrelevant because of our rigidly whipped party system – almost unique except for puppet parliaments in one party states. A 'whipped' voting system is where nominated representatives ensure all members vote according to the collectively agreed position of their party. It can be a thoroughly democratic and efficient means of effecting legislation. Indeed, without some discipline parliamentary debates would get out of control or Parliament would deadlock. What is different about the Australian system is its intensity and rigidity: there is always a 'three-line' whip in place. There is never room for deviation – if you break the line you lose the whip and may well be expelled from your party. Now, if there is a place for genuine debate within party caucuses there might be reason to be happy with this system. However, there is never genuine caucus debate because the major parties usually only meet for an hour a week. There is barely enough time to read out the decisions made elsewhere – so there can be no possibility of genuine constructive discussion. Caucus members rarely get more than a one-page note on any given bill and are often oblivious to what they are voting on (witness the Liberals voting to go along with John Howard's rear-guard action on MPs' super in early 2004).

Some Cabinets are little better. Advisers have such control over information relevant to particular decision-making processes that it's mostly impossible to out-debate them on principle, let alone fact. If that's the reality of life as a Cabinet member, is it any wonder Federal and State Oppositions find it so hard to get governments on the back foot these days.

Under the rigidly whipped system you can't express or mobilise dissent at these processes. You shut down. You might introduce a private member's bill – but there are so few opportunities to debate these that the course of action is limited and rarely produces a successful outcome. Most private member's bills come from minor parties and independents. These privileges are often an indulgence exchanged in return for other cooperation when they hold the balance of power in a particular upper house.

Recently the Senate has proved effective at reviewing government legislation. Yet, fundamentally, instead of being a showcase of the diversity and drive that exists in political parties or a repository of expertise and wisdom, like the UK's House of Lords, it is a warehouse for clapped-out officials, sanctimonious moral high grounders, and the rotten end of backroom transactions. With the government now in full control of the Senate, its underlying feebleness will be exposed. Without the numbers against the government the Senate will be as impotent as it is lacking in real skill. And the Senate is the cream. If we were to analyse the state upper houses here, I'd have to slit my wrists.

In his own damning way the Clerk of the Senate, Harry Evans, warns us all what path this mediocrity promised us:

> The prime minister determines how the electors' representatives vote ... the governor-general is hired and fired by the prime minister; the prime minister, who is the executive government, controls the House

of Representatives ... the federal government has been able to take over virtually any state functions; High Court judges are appointed by the prime minister with regard to their ideological persuasion. But what does the Parliament do? he would ask. Answer: members act as a cheer squad for their leader.[4]

On another level there is a chronic lack of thought and effort among the relevant people in the ALP, Democrats and Greens – the parties of the centre and left – for figuring out how they might better work together. Intent on feathering their own nest, the party strategists fail to recognise how the lack of mature working relationships between the opposition parties fails us all.

Progressive young voters should be able to know that as a general principle these three parties will work together and for election purposes run a tight preferencing circle. Coalition voters get that via a different arrangement, but they get it. The outward signs of such a mature public relationship could include things like regular meetings between the respective party leaderships and something more than the frantic and botched last-minute attempts at preference deals during election campaigns themselves. Such actions would be examples of how politicians can take the public seriously.

But fundamentally, the structure of politics in Australia does not require the public to be involved in any meaningful way. There are so many people employed in government-funded, yet deeply partisan political positions that all politics can be organised without the participation of keen voters or party rank-and-file. Television advertisements can be bought by the bucket load in election campaigns and this is simpler than organizing 5000 people to simultaneously knock on front doors. No one measures whether this is effective, and no one has the guts to ask the question. It's an addiction that suits the comfortable cliques that run the significant political parties, but like all addictions there are victims – and in this instance the victims happen to be us. An unfortunate downside of our genial compulsory preferential voting system is that it reinforces the lack of active engagement with the electorate and allows those in political circles to continue on in their detached and self-referencing world. For every Garrett or Turnbull there are a dozen time-servers, wannabe MPs and artless lackeys without the life experience, challenging opinions and strategies necessary to make our federal Parliament worthy of the people in whose name it rules.[5] That we have a layer of state governments means we have nine of these political elites instead of one, and the tide of talent is out for all of them. When younger people see all this it is a magnetic repellant to involvement in institutional politics, and the magnetic force simply draws them deeper and deeper into the world of NGOs or their iPods. It is a mess of mediocrity that will take more than my generation to fix.

The Greens are not the new black

For several years from 2001 the Australian Greens were white-hot. As appealing as Natasha Stott-Despoja was before them but to a more deeply political set. Their appeal wasn't limited to one generation but was especially strong amongst the young. The appeal isn't white-hot these days, but it's still more than lukewarm. And that's deeply depressing for those who care about results more than rhetoric.

Activism is not a form of therapy. Nor is personal gain the reason to become politically active. If you are pressing for global or local change in society for either of those reasons you are indulging a serious personality flaw. The only result of these actions is long-term harm to others.

Too often, activism and its crippled sibling the 'protest vote' are about helping individuals clamber onto the moral high ground to perform a one-person martyrdom pantomime. Voting for the Greens is the classic recent example. Few people who vote Green can articulate exactly why, beyond the muttered 'conviction': 'They're

PLEASE JUST F* OFF . . . IT'S OUR TURN NOW

the only ones who say what I believe'. 'At least you know where you stand' is another refrain. So what? You don't vote to make yourself feel better – it's not chocolate. And since when did knowing where you stood fix complex social problems? People knew where they stood with Jeff Kennett – and where did that get them? Clarity is no substitute for substance, and that is a mistake the faux-activist often makes. If you're a real activist you do things because they help make a difference not because you want to feel better.

I contend that in their current state the Australian Greens party is a force *against* seriousness on the Left/progressive side of politics in Australia.

> Voting for the Greens has become this manifestation of the attitude that nothing you do has to change – you can just vote for the Greens because they stand for the improbable.

That's how one 29-year-old Labor supporter raged at me over coffee in trendy Surry Hills. She *would* say that. But not having to do anything about your life to make the world better seems to be a common thread running through a lot of Green political activity in our inner cities. Privileged people have simply become adept at protecting their lot and now have the Greens to speak for them.

The people I am talking about want mobility and luxury rather than worldwide social justice. A few might donate to refugee charities but they would have second thoughts (actually, they'd be really pissed) if those refugees moved into a purpose-built block of flats across the road and bumped their Rav4's from their precious car spaces (don't tell them *The Economist* reckons that in New York 'nearly half of all new housing in the past seven years is reckoned to be occupied by immigrants or their children').[6] They accept the radical social justice rhetoric of the Greens because these views will never affect their lifestyle while the Green's benign local government policies – all about enhancing their local lifestyles

– will. Anything that encroaches on this pampered lifestyle is called 'over-development'. The Greens can get away with this because their behaviour has not been subject to proper scrutiny. It's eerily similar to how the Australian Democrats used to look warm and friendly before the GST – and we know what happened to them. I dare not suggest Australian Greens Party members are anything but energetic. There may be many examples of individual Greens councillors who work harder than their counterparts from the major parties. But their efforts don't affect my overall structural critique and shouldn't stop us correcting the public mythology about their party.

Problems with Labor

Labor's very essence is what is holding it back from making the great leap forward into 21st century political reality. Labor has a control problem. Its appointees, union affiliates and icons pretty much all want control. But the narrative of 21st century life is the opposite of a controlled environment. It is impossible to make complete sense of, let alone control, anything beyond your immediate sphere in our extremely complex and turbo-charged world. Whether it's unions trying to control the party platform, the machinery trying to control the rank-and-file, the leaking rats who try and control public perception of the party's processes – the causes and symptoms are the same. Until the ALP lets its hair down and focuses on the electoral niche markets that splatter our political landscape it can forget about capturing our imaginations. The party has become a last refuge for authoritarian personalities and loyalist flunkies who can't get a gig elsewhere in a changing world. I say this as someone who gave up two years of my working life and the better part of the social life of my late teens and early twenties to this party. I don't regret that, but it's impossible not to feel cheated by this carcass of a party that, like Australia, could be so much more. If it doesn't wake up the only

Five myths about The Greens

1 That the Greens Party is above politics.

Beneath the veneer of Saint Bob Brown dozens of smaller, uglier faces exist. Jeremy Buckingham, a Greens councillor near Orange in NSW is a good example. Just so you know he is still a 'normal' bloke he told the *Sunday Telegraph* 'I'm not a vegetarian and I'm also heterosexual'.[7] Phew. That's the last thing we need: more carrot-eating gays in politics! I mean there's probably at least three of them now. I did, however, wonder what Ray Goodlass – the next person interviewed and at the time a new Wagga Wagga councillor – would have thought about Buckingham's joke. You see, Ray and I appeared on a panel at an international trade union conference in 2002 – for gay and lesbian trade unionists.

Buckingham's defensive and opportunistic comment is a tip-off. The Greens aren't saints and aren't necessarily clever – just like other political parties.

2 That the Greens Party is really left-wing.

'There is a tendency to conservatize when in power, but I'm sure we will stick by the policies we were elected on.' So says Geoff Ash, NSW Greens co-convenor. Sure. But what policies are they sticking to? Buckingham for one thinks a bizarre alliance can be formed with conservative farmers over genetically modified foods – 'on a lot of issues we are saying the same things. Or at least we are saying what the National Party used to say.' Great. So the Greens are just stealing old ideas and turning back the clock in a reactionary attempt to claim a political niche? Hmmm. At least Labor doesn't pretend it is pure.

3 That the Greens Party is 'grassroots'.

Just how grassroots can a party be when almost half of its candidates in the 2004 Queensland state election didn't even live in the electorate for which they were a candidate? To me that smells like an opportunistic party machine slotting people into seats on the last day of nominations to increase the state-wide vote. If you support having no local infrastructure to deliver on any promise made by a ring-in candidate – then consider voting Green. Oh, and don't mention a certain multinational beauty products company whose profits make a major contribution to party funds in NSW.

4 That there are no factions in the Greens Party.

When questioning a paid employee of the Greens party in New South Wales I was told that the party isn't being taken over by socialists – the so-called 'red-green' or 'watermelon' members of the party. No, according to this hack, these people are simply 'justice-driven'. Did I say hack? Sorry, I meant activist. You see The Greens Party don't have hacks. Just like they don't have General Secretaries or Leaders. They have Convenors and Spokespeople. They don't chair meetings, Senator Kerry Nettle once told me, they facilitate them. These distinctions aren't meaningless – they can validly describe important functions in the activist world. The problem is, they can't describe what political parties do, and that's what The Greens Party is. They have factions and they are a machine like Labor and the Liberals. The fact they turn people out on every polling booth while Democrats 'how to vote' cards sit under rocks and on unstaffed card tables is evidence of that machine. It's time The Greens Party came clean on more than their power industry policies.

5 The Greens Party don't do deals.

Election analyst Anthony Green knows that's nonsense – having publicly stated how both the Democrats and Greens are very deal savvy. Indeed, The Greens' only Sydney Mayor ever – Murray Matson in Waverley – got that position because of a deal with Liberals. Don't mention that Senator Kerry Nettle got elected off One Nation preferences either – because then you might have to accept the Greens negotiate and compromise and sell themselves into more preference deals than any other party.

thing the Labor party will be controlling is its own demise.

It is rather odd and sad to think that the Liberal party is more diverse and inclusive than the Labor party – a fact confirmed by a quick look at its parliamentary ranks. Labor may talk the talk on these issues but the talentless rump of a federal parliamentary caucus whose many no-hopers and clapped-out hacks suffocate the party's few fresh and talented faces speaks much louder than Labor's words. Whereas the Howard Government has grown stronger in its capabilities, the Labor Opposition is weaker. Caucus members would do well to think more about their obituaries than tomorrow's headlines. Until they do Labor will remain a deadbeat culture disengaged from the ideas and methods of the creative and independently successful people it needs to attract to its caucus, membership and support base.

As I write, attention is now turning to Baby Boomer nostalgia for the 30th anniversary of the Whitlam dismissal. But why concentrate on the future when you can get drunk on the past? The parallel problem is while some generations cannot look past the past, others have absolutely no sense of it.

While much of this book argues for more involvement of young people in public life there is one exception – political representation and advice, something I've had genuine experience of. On several occasions I have spoken at conferences or to groups who feel that one problem with our political system is that there aren't more young MPs. I reject that view. I don't want to throw young MPs out; they do add diversity to our parliaments. However, the primary challenge of engaging young people with democracy is certainly not to get more young MPs – getting young people to enrol to vote is a far more important start. Secondly, how can one claim to represent the whole community – the purpose of being an MP – if you have had no real experience of living beyond the youth wing of your party and the university bar? You needn't have worked in public, private and voluntary sectors, have been a parent, lived rich and poor, in three states and have celebrated your 50th birthday to be an MP, but with few exceptions you do need at least a few of those experiences to be legitimate and successful. That is something most 25-year-olds can't do, and it is what marks this profession as different to one where you follow a rigid procedure or simply try to increase sales of widget X or gadget Y.

Which brings me to the ongoing problem of people who think that they can be good political advisers or union officials after two years of university activism. With the benefit of both hindsight and the good sense to get out of the game when it became apparent to me, I firmly believe you just can't do a good job as a political adviser without lengthy experience of our diverse world. A short stint as a political researcher or electorate officer while completing a degree or TAFE course might be fine. But having to deal with big and complex delivery departments, billions of dollars and dozens of meritorious but competing stakeholders is a tough challenge for anyone. To suggest that someone in their early- or mid-twenties who has neither worked in a 'real' full time job, nor worked in an industry that they claim to be able to represent, can do it well is almost laughable. Our democracy is much poorer for this misconception.

There are thousands of well-qualified and independent-minded people who can do these jobs. It is a crime against democracy that too often these jobs go, in the absence of open competition, to people from particular friendship networks and factional cliques who, if they are as good as they think they are, would have the good sense to wait until they are closer to or beyond 30 before applying for such posts.

To think that we have advanced the cause of my generation by seizing control of the political advice elite is not progressive. It is to witness a false dawn that obscures the much more real and grassroots changes that we need to make to our democracy better.

PLEASE JUST F* OFF . . . IT'S OUR TURN NOW

Unions

A key lesson the union movement needs to learn is that if it can't find out new issues and movements before it's competitors (bosses, the Liberals, whatever) do, then the results of those issues will be forced down its throat. You'd think the economic restructuring of the 1980s was a good warning in that respect.

Work/life balance is one issue where unions have actually been going around lighting a few fires, making us think about the world of work differently. But even that movement has struggled to capture the public mood and young people aren't enamoured with the concept.[8] Why unions think they can cut in the 21st century or qualify as 'radical' because they have adopted campaigns around work/life balance is beyond me. What do they think the eight-hour day was all about? We've been there and done that a century and a half ago. Of course it should be defended, and using the new label 'work/life balance' if necessary, but this should happen as a matter of course. Whining that the pressures and expectations on employees in the 21st century are greater than ever doesn't bear thinking about. That's what everyone in 21st century advanced capitalism lives with.

In any case, I don't want a mandated 35-hour week. I like being at work. It stimulates me, improves me and I enjoy the time I have with my colleagues. If I enjoy it, why shouldn't I be allowed to do it? I want control of my life, rather than someone else telling me I have to treat work and home life as if they were irreconcilable. I don't give a toss if my standard work day is seven hours or seven hours and 12 minutes or even eight hours. I care about being able to come in late if I am looking after someone who is ill or after a big night out. The right to work from home if I need to crack on with a project or don't feel well is important. I don't want surveillance of my every move in the office and I need the right to take two days off at short notice if it is time to recharge my batteries. In short, I care about 'time sovereignty' – the right to dictate which hours are worked, not how many there are.[9] Some jobs inherently can't allow that flexibility – you can't run a checkout from your bed or pluck a chicken from the sofa. But many skilled blue-collar workers have left the big corporate work shops to set up as self-employed tradies so this is a broadly applicable trend. They do it so they can control their own hours, pick their kids up from school, play some sport or do a course. Comprehending those desires means accepting that contracts can deliver the freedom from the boss that strikes, nationalisation, and socialism failed to achieve. These manual workers want the same freedom as the intelligentsia take for granted. John Howard understands this and so do most young people. Unions need to stop worrying about how all these different ways of working makes it harder for them to organise and accept that these are the people they need to adapt to.

Changing from issues to mediums, it's instructive to look at online organising. Unions worldwide are successfully cracking this nut while in Australia the rigid bureaucracies of individual unions prevail over the hard work and vision of a small minority. www.workSMART.org.uk is a website open to all comers giving advice and support whether you are a member of a union or not – indeed 'especially non-union members.'[10] It is incumbent upon unions who want to think of their members and prospective members rather than their own institutional interests to consider other dramatic changes in the way they operate. These must include allowing peer-to-peer networking at all levels of the union movement. That is, setting up opt-in directories so that union members can contact each other as they choose. This would build connectivity and allow members to form useful relationships for their own benefit and that of the wider movement. If it works for university alumni associations and schoolfriends.com.au then it can work for unions.

In the cut-throat economy of the 21st century you live or die by who you know and who the people you know know. It's as true for home-based hairdressers as it is for communications consultants.

Access to professional networks falls into the category of 'bridging social capital' – social capital that takes you to different and better places through the new information and relationships it provides. Unions will stagnate without strategies to build and distribute this resource.

Accredited training such as vocational, diploma and degree courses could be a goldmine. I often wonder why the ACTU does not set up an online university delivering itself, its members and the nation a service in one hit. If religious denominations can set up educational institutions then so can trade unions – self improvement is a powerful and popular message and should be at the heart of their pitch to members. It's also reclaiming private education for a better purpose than giving dumb rich kids good jobs.

Unions don't think that training people to do their jobs is part of their business. But if that's what their members want and it's a market from which they can make money – then it's a lesson they have to learn. Unions might think MBAs are something nasty management types have – but they are actually something their own potential members want. Having a rewarding professional career today is about perpetual personal development. Skills and qualifications are now inseparable from old style pay and conditions issues, and without them you won't have a job in the globalised economy. Even the phrase 'lifelong learning' doesn't cover the concept anymore. It is about self-directed learning, formal qualifications, regular updating of key skills and developing a series of generic capabilities in fields such as communication and management that allow you to cope in stressful, new environments.

The politics I've written about in this chapter are the politics of the 20th century. The people of this century don't need them, and increasingly they're saying they don't want them. What's the answer? There is no single answer – but without innovation we won't even find part of the collection of answers we need. Without

Are trade unions failing young people?

A cultural tide has swept the country that dwarfs the Waterfront dispute or individual contracts in terms of significance. Ask anyone under 30 what unions are and what they should do and we answer to a different tune from our parents. Unions are not understood and are not part of the political furniture. They are an oddity you read about in tabloids and economics textbooks.

About two million Australians aged 15–24 participate in the workforce, 66 percent of them on a casual basis, the majority in retail and food service. The next biggest group is in well-paid jobs like property and business services. We have a generation of young workers oblivious to unions in comfortable well-paid jobs or difficult to organise casual jobs. To put it in figures, just 11.6 percent of 15–19-year-olds are in unions.[11] Most of these belong to the Shop, Distributive and Allied Employees Association (SDA). The SDA does virtually nothing to involve its members in defending their wages and conditions and absolutely nothing of relevance to the wider social concerns of its members. It fuels a culture of complete non-engagement with unions.

In 2002 ACTU Assistant Secretary Richard Marles told the first ACTU Youth Conference: 'the union movement will die if we cannot attract young people'. He's right. The ACTU faces an annual $300 million back hole in its members' budgets if it cannot increase its appeal to the current under-thirties. Many unionists know this but rarely speak about it. The frustration is not limited to particular factions or states either – it operates on a generational axis.

new strategies to overcome the wedge issues dividing our society we won't ever move forward. There is now an opportunity to stop talking about the disaffection that has been talked about so much, and to start doing something about it. That's the opportunity presented by the need for generational change.

PART THREE

It's time Boomers

TOMORROW can be better than today, and everyone has a personal, moral responsibility to make it so.
Professor Carroll Quigley[1]

I never see what has been done; I only see what remains to be done.
Marie Curie

CONVICTION is contagious; never underestimate the power of persistence.
Nelson Mandela

CHAPTER TWELVE

The future is now

Now that we have seen what is different and good about my generation juxtaposed with Australian under-achievement, the question is: what are we going to do to improve Australia?

Even nostalgic Richard Neville admits 'you can't go on believing the same things forever'. And thank God for that – because we mustn't continue believing everything is fine. It's not. We're no basket case, the threat of the banana republic never ripened, but we can certainly do better.

We could change structurally – by picking sectors or fields and remoulding them, or inventing and establishing whole new organisations. We could make cultural change by shaping new ways of doing things, generating new shared understandings. We can seek emotional responses – by striking fear into people or inspiring blind loyalty to a person or cause. And we can do it by renewal – getting new people to do the things that need doing, separate from the question of whether they are actually the right things to do.

It strikes me that what Australia needs most is a combination of the second and fourth strategies outlined above. We need a new and hopeful cultural mindset and we need it to be enabled by a process of renewal. Yes, we can change the structures and institutions and that will bear some fruit. Yes, we need to be able to generate emotional responses to make people want to care about democracy and community. But it is only by really changing the way people view their country and their role in renewing it that dramatic change can be achieved.

I could promise dazzling visions and the Fourth Way, but we don't need false prophets or a re-sloganing of the same old junk. In the words of 22-year-old Simon Moss from Melbourne: 'the ideas that drove the baby boomer generation just aren't feasible. We're not going to subscribe to one big idea. The 20th century was a disaster trying to achieve one big idea.' It follows that we do not need a false certainty, but new conditions and a new mindset to foster new people and new ideas, properly rewarded and resourced, to reinvigorate our country. We must be radical. Radical without always confusing radical with left wing.

The future is now

My generation will be aged 30 to 45 by the time the deadline for the United Nation's Millennium Development Goals bitch slaps us in 2015. They were agreed to by 147 heads of state in 2000 – but it is up to my generation to deliver them. Given inevitabilities like this, it makes sense to embed us in decision-making now.

The alternative to a smooth generational handover is a divided society overly dependent on two sets of cosmopolitan elites. The first will be the home-grown set who leave periodically to access opportunities and the second will be the overseas, mostly Asian, student base who are sucked in and bled dry for a few years and disposed of when their presence is no longer convenient. ('Universities need about 220,000 foreign students a year to stay financially viable.'[2]) We are better off building a future on a broader, more democratic base than that.

Why it is important to take a risk on young people

It was Albert Einstein who said we can't solve problems by using the same kind of thinking we used when we created them. Adopting a 21st-century version of this attitude involves risk, failed ideas and lost money, but innovation comes from all these things and is surely what we must aim for.

I can't remember the number of ideas I've had for activist campaigns that didn't work the first time, but which I later used to good effect. Those experiences instilled in me the firm belief that new ideas have to 'put out there'. Doing so means smarter people in the right place at a better time can use them to greater effect, and companies and governments as well as young individuals have a responsibility to help make this possible.

Ask yourself these questions if you remain unconvinced. Will Australia be more united if we ignore generational tensions? Do you really believe half a generation of people will be happy never to own a home?

And precisely what is scary about generational change, anyway? That's what a globalised world is all about. You can't live in the 21st century and suddenly decide you don't like change. That's not how modernity works. There is an information revolution, a consumer orgy, a war on terror, and the rapid integration of more than 200 nation states all whirling around us. You can't stop this rollercoaster because a few people in their fifties in Australia are done with change and want to enjoy the view for a little longer.

Now is the time for other generations to jump on our bandwagon – leave it any longer and it will be too late to take some of the credit or share the spoils of what we are able to generate. You will be so last season. And it will be a long dry season for you. I see this trend in dozens of initiatives that are starting to shift from common 'flash in the pan' or fringe fad into the realms of serious organisations and projects. Several of these have received a showcase in earlier chapters – ReconciliACTION, The Oaktree Foundation, the Foundation of Young Professionals, and **notgoodenough.org** all meet this criteria. Breakthroughs are happening in the strangest places – from bank managers getting younger, to the Australian version of America's *Moveon* – **www.getup.org.au** – to magazine start-ups like *Lip*, *Stu* and *Yen* and *Vibewire* (slogan: 'The voices of our generation will not be ignored').[3] These youth media groups not only have an annual professional youth media festival *Noise*, they act 'as a canary in the cultural coal mine, their styles and stories later copied by publishing, cinema and, in particular, television'.[4] There are email lists like YouthGAS and institutional hangovers like the network of National Youth Roundtable alumni also seething with economies of intellectual scale. The YWCA has done what almost all of its religious counterparts have failed to do and successfully engaged with its target audiences and the community rather than lecturing, converting or corrupting them. We see fledgling attempts at intellectual renaissance too. There is the OzPropsect 'think tank', the Imagining Australia Foundation, the Foundation for Young Australians, and those old hard nuts the student unions who refuse to die in the face of the Coalition's Voluntary Student Unionism policies. None of them is dependent on government funds like most of the old stalwart activist groups from decades past.

When I think back to how, as a member of the first National Youth Roundtable in 1999 I despaired of our responsibilities in the wake of the forced collapse of the youth peak body AYPAC, I can only respond by chuckling inside. I and many others on the Roundtable thought millions of young Australian would be voiceless and ignored with only the 50 of us as a final barricade defending the 'voice of youth'. How wrong we were. We underestimated the resilience of young people in such a hostile environment. From the clearer perspective of 2006 it's obvious there are bright spots and determined people who will patch together what is needed for a changing of the guard. These people will not be random individuals, so much as a wave. You might not yet see it – just as a tsunami can pass you unnoticed in the deep ocean. But you will notice when that wave comes crashing down on your doorstep in the next decade. It's passing under you now.

New language is where it starts

The first step to a new mindset is new language. It's not post-modern clap trap that's called for, but language must be the starting point as it's our best tool for making and expressing the meaning of the world around us.

I read with regret a book titled *Imagining Australia*. Written by four thirty-ish Australians fresh out of a Harvard scholarship stint and published in 2004, *Imagining Australia* smelt of compromise in its weakest sense. For sure the authors are part of an emerging intellectual backlash against the people and institutions that are stifling this country but they were insufficiently radical in their approach. They spoke of redefining the project of 'nation-building' and re-asserting 'egalitarianism, mateship and the fair go'. It sounds nice – but we don't need re-interpretations of old ideas.

To my delight, one of the authors of *Imagining Australia*, David Madden, has gone on to become a founder of the fantastic and radical **getup.org.au** campaign group.

We need to both set an example for future generations and seize today a fair share of power and wealth for ourselves. This requires new approaches and new language – two of our strengths. My proposition that we should forget nation-building and think 'glue issues' is a pertinent example. The point is to dream of what will make Australia great in the 21st century not to pine for another version of what made it vibrant in the 20th. Reclaiming language and concepts that have been stolen by conservatives from progressive people is not the best answer. That theft tells us that these old concepts embedded in tightly controlled notions of group solidarity like 'mateship' and 'nation-building' are now conservative. Progressive politics are by definition new, and will be imagined and set free by new words.

The evolution of language is therefore an essential starting point to a generational changeover in Australia. Without new language it will also not be possible to make all of the beneficiaries aware of when and how change is taking place. Without new language we cannot truly *own* a generational transition because it will be taking place on someone else's terms. And it will be harder for the beneficiaries of the changeover to participate and they will be less likely to embrace its outcomes. We need new language now.

Dialogue, not lectures

The importance of new language to generational change is not merely about words, it is about the structure and setting of their use. *Australian Idol* and *Big Brother* work for two reasons: they are completely transparent and because the whole thing is a gigantic conversation – the type we never get to have with traditional institutions and powerbrokers. '(If I were a politician) . . . I would actually converse with people instead of talking at them', is how Rachel Hills, 24, puts it.

Looking at our two-party system dividing along the insufficient lines of 'left' and 'right' we must ask: what's special or different about political ideologies that should cause them to be immune to radical overhaul? Our political and activist elite will happily renew everything else in their life from swim-wear fashion to technology; yet when it comes to political views they insist on super-gluing themselves to the past. Binary concepts like left and right and the stigma that goes with them are a turn off. The concepts are everything people of my generation are not. We make thousands of choices every day in our lives. They can't all be pigeon-holed into left or right. While the deception persists that narrow ideologies can describe a diverse reality we can bet on a further slide in the institutions of liberal democracy. Whether it's the Pope or Lenin the advocates of such nonsense will be faced with derision. Alternatively we could start serious and ongoing discussion about what innovations might actually help us out of our mess.

IT is not the critic who counts, not the man who points out how the strong man stumbled, or where the doer of deeds could have done better. The credit belongs to the man who is actually in the arena; whose face is marred by the dust and sweat and blood; who strives valiantly . . . who at the best, knows in the end the triumph of high achievement, and who, at the worst, if he fails, at least fails while daring greatly; so that his place shall never be with those cold and timid souls who know neither victory nor defeat.

Theodore Roosevelt

THE historical way of developing products just doesn't work when you're as ambitious as we are.

Ive (no last name)
Industrial Design Chief for Apple

CHAPTER THIRTEEN

Doing It

My generation will know we've screwed it up if we behave like the Boomers and fail to deliver on our promises. We must be the realistic, responsible generation that admits to the problems our society faces, commits to taking on the challenge of fixing them, and is honest about our progress.

In changing society we must ourselves be prepared to change. This means adopting and shedding ideas when it's appropriate and sharing, not hogging, power. Boomers aren't irrelevant and shouldn't and won't accept pointless marginalisation, nor will they simply hand over the keys to society. The challenge therefore is to shift them to one side rather than throw them overboard.

There are essential strategies we have to adopt before that will take place. The first is developing an improved collective self-belief. The second is a commitment to rebuilding trust. The third and most important is a passion for innovation. The last – implementing decent citizenship education – is the platform for developing a new democracy and the glue issues (discussed in Chapter 14) that might bind Australians together again.

As if

One of the most important things I've ever learnt to do is to live 'as if' – 'as if' something exists when it doesn't. It's not universal and I didn't think it up, but it's brilliant.[1] Acting 'as if' is sometimes the only way to keep your spirits up when things seem hopeless. You need self-belief to live 'as if' and then it becomes self-perpetuating. I swear by it because it's fundamentally true that no one can force you to stop thinking particular things. 'As if' you have a right to make personal phone calls from work if you are the carer for an unwell person; 'as if' it's practical to ride your bike around the city because if enough people did it would be. If you can't live 'as if' then you allow your idea to die. When living 'as if' is done alone it's easy to be ignored or dismissed. When enough people live 'as if' that's when cultural change becomes possible. Living 'as if' means you are armed and ready when the crossfire of a generational conflict breaks out. War is not 24/7 – there's lots of dead time – but you have to be ready for the action.

Eliminating the freak factor

Passive mindsets, once in place, are not easy to change. In Australia's case we aren't John Howard's fantastical 'relaxed and comfortable', we're just comfortably numb. It's easier to give into this mindset than to change it and it will take time to reverse that imbalance.

It is incumbent now upon all those who value what young Australians have to offer to change our current mindset. Both bravery and brains are needed. Speaking out is important. Do it now. Just getting your audience – at the dinner table, in your classroom or in the national media – to a position where they can conceive that you could have something useful to say is the immediate goal. As a start we'd welcome the reaction of our favourite Fountain Lakes resident Kath Day-Knight during 'wine time': 'interesting . . . but I don't agree.' Getting people to admit you have a germ of an idea is a relatively easy strategy to defend. They might disagree with the scale of the complaint or explain how it doesn't apply to them personally, but they can't argue with the fact that Baby Boomers own more property than any other generation, dominate our media and have their arses glued to the parliamentary benches. That said, if the particular idea in question is crap it won't go anywhere, but take comfort from the legendary *Washington Post* publisher Katharine Graham: 'when an idea is right, nothing can stop it.'[2] Our good ideas will gain momentum and we can use this fact as an opening to achieve generational equity and a better Australia.

Rebuilding trust

Without renewed trust the institutions of our society will falter then fail. Rebuilding trust needs to be at the forefront of your thinking.

Trust is fragile in our marketplaces because of poor corporate governance, uncompetitive markets and exploitation. Trust is lacking in politics because our people are not educated about what the state really can and cannot do and our politicians rarely have honest and lengthy conversations with the public. People mistrust our media because it fluctuates between irrelevant adversarialism, a lust for gross things and a benign absence of thought and investigation – all fuelled by a lack of creative and competitive tension. One cure is to take risks. The other part of solution is to pass the baton on to those who will ultimately have to bridge the 'trust gap' – the people born after 1970.

PLEASE JUST F* OFF . . . IT'S OUR TURN NOW

I-N-N-O-V-A-T-I-O-N – spell it with me

IF I had asked people what they wanted, they would have said faster horses.

Henry Ford

Innovation is a buzz word that littered a decade of government policy papers. There are Innovation Strategies, Innovation Plans, Departments for Innovation, and Innovation Start-Up Schemes. So why don't I feel more Innovated? Why does public life feel dull and uninspiring?

I'm very happy to make mistakes. In fact, I think mistakes are a good thing. If telling others about my mistakes encourages them to make their own then that pleases me immensely. It's not that I like wasting resources or have a fetish for failure – I just know it's the best way to learn. It's not about 'learning the hard way' – it's about self-confidence and self-improvement. The voting population clinging to John Howard and the Labor Party returning to Kim Beazley is just sad – it's not learning or changing anything, and we will come to regret it. History will not be kind to the current leaders of Australia for squandering our prosperity and urging us to live like there is no tomorrow.

Electing Mark Latham as a leader was not a mistake, even if that particular process didn't succeed. It was a break from the past and that is surely a progressive thing. But conservatism won out in what is supposed to be a progressive organisation. The chiefs of the ALP have forgotten that most ideas don't work first time round. Latham's failure cannot equal the end of change, the sidestepping of regeneration. Set against the context of the real world around us it's naïve and irresponsible to think that retreating to the likes of Kim Beazley will fix any underlying problem with that side of politics.

Rather 'risks are a measure of people. People who won't take them are trying to preserve what they have'.[3] And from that we can extrapolate that unless you take risks on young people and their ideas then innovation can never happen on a large scale. Think of what would have happened if **Amazon.com** has taken the same attitude as the ALP – would it be a juggernaut, or even here, today? Think of the number of ideas out there we are ignoring when instead we ought to be testing and learning and profiting from them.

The Dotcom bubble was genuine innovation followed by minor catastrophe. Forget the collapse of One-Tel and listen briefly to the key point the co-founder of **lastminute.com** took from that era: 'There was a community of young people starting businesses.' The Dotcom bubble was a major learning curve that gave birth to thousands of ideas and entrepreneurs who are now able to apply their experiences for personal and collective good. Sean Howard who created OzEmail and sold it seven years later in 1999 for $520 million is a case in point.[4] At the other end of the spectrum Simba Textiles, recently Australia's smallest towel manufacturer, has used open source web platforms to become the world leader in the personalised towel market. At a macro level in 2006, all but very specific microbusinesses have strategies of clicks and mortar rather than bricks and mortar. Whatever way you cut it, the e-commerce explosion is a systemic endorsement of the Dotcom era and the willingness of its players to take risks.

Instead of sweeping that era away as proof that young people were unable to deliver, it's time to recognise that we actually need much more of that spirit applied, of course, in sustainable ways.

How quickly can we change?

The Industrial Revolution took half a century to take hold in Great Britain and be spread to other nations. The so called Tiger Economies in Asia transformed themselves in 20–30 years and were considered to have done so at breakneck speed.

We are at a distinct advantage in this regard because we don't need to start a way of working from scratch – we just need to mobilise and exploit something that is already there: young people and their ideas. My generation has a great capacity to think laterally and cope with today's complex environments, as I have outlined in Part One. So we can change and we can do it relatively quickly if we foster a culture that supports innovation.[5]

Where is the Harbour Bridge of the 21st century? Where is the new Opera House? I'd rather not think in terms of the 'new Opera House' – there must be something completely original but different out there that could capture our spirits just as well. But we can't even built a fast train connecting Canberra to the outside world!

Innovation is the introduction of completely new ideas or methods and exploiting them.[6] We can't succeed in a rapidly changing world by simply tweaking what we've already got. It's not about doing what we already do now, except on a website. Improvements to old ideas – like business models that make flights or eating out cheaper – may improve living standards, but they do not make us dynamic.

Under the umbrella of improving our democracy here are three distinct examples of innovation involving different groups using different tactics for equally important outcomes:

1. To improve democracy in the short term we need innovative activism.
2. To provide medium term change we need innovative workplaces.
3. To provide the long term platform for ongoing democracy we need excellent citizenship education in our school system.

Innovation and democracy

Phrases like 'innovation' and 'excellence' are nearly always used in reference to a technological or business venture. It's telling that we had a National Office of the Innovation Economy (NOIE) funded by the federal government, but no equivalent body looking at more fundamental concepts like our democracy. Even the failed constitutional referendums of 1988 and 1999 were more about grandees grandstanding than participatory, radical or useful. No wonder they failed. Who needs external terrorists to attack democracy? We can do it perfectly well ourselves by ignoring it.

The factors behind the declining faith in parliamentary democracy link to innovation and generational change in several ways. Firstly, we are told that the generations before us achieved almost all the important changes that our society needed as preconditions for a civilised and egalitarian world. Anything we try to do – we're told they did it better. This is terrible for democracy because it reinforces the sense of futility that many have with the democratic process. Why would you bother if there's nothing left to change and you are no good at it anyway?

Secondly, there has been an inevitable narrowing of political choices with the elimination of competitors to capitalism. Now there are fewer places to turn for political comfort. Some socialist viewpoints have been exposed as weak or simply wrong. There are more parties than ever fighting over the remaining turf. We have achieved political consensus on previously vexing issues. So let's get on with creating an agenda for *this* century.

All Australians have been brought up with poor or non-existent citizenship education. No wonder interest in parliamentary democracy is slipping further from our collective grasp. Inevitable? No. Bad for democracy? Definitely.

If Boomers find their second wind by giving a louder voice to the 'Grey Power' movement as they stack their numbers into that demographic we'll be sorry we didn't stamp on it now. A significant minority of my generation will simply turn their back on government and our civil society. Living in a foreign country has taught me how easy it is to cope without government. I don't visit doctors, I don't have a clue how to file a tax return, nor do I know the frequency of public radio stations. Now that I ride a bike I only use public transport on a semi-regular basis. I fear that one day we will wake up and realise that millions of my generation have also absconded from the public realm simply because we can and because no one made decent arguments to us about why we shouldn't. That's what rich, educated people can do these days and there will be more who can in my generation than ever before. If and as that happens it will be very tempting for politicians of all ages to continue their descent into pork-barrelling the loyal Baby Boomers.

It's not too late to care about democracy and generational equity. If we can have all manner of incentives and tax breaks for casinos and mining companies don't tell me we can't afford democratic initiatives like citizenship education. Think of what millions of extra dollars would do for projects that spread democratic tools and strengthen communities. Where are our efforts to hand more control of schools and neighbourhood facilities to the local consumers? Where is the money from the Commonwealth Grants Commission to encourage grassroots proposals to do so?

We need to stop congratulating ourselves on being a parliamentary democracy. The challenge for 21st century is to deepen democracy.

Innovative activism

The 'New Mardi Gras' organisation in Sydney is a model in its efforts to be inclusive of and relevant to young people and the wider community. Young people are viewed within the organisation as the 'future of Mardi Gras' and this is reflected across its activities. When the organisation was sent into bankruptcy in 2002, caused by an aging, out of touch and cliquey leadership, a resurrection was led by two women in their twenties and two men in their early thirties.

> THE old Mardi Gras was particularly exclusive. It was about being rich and white and inner city. The board presented things to you on a platter. The New Mardi Gras is better because there is more community control. You can be 20

and be interested and go on a committee and present an idea about something that should happen at the party and it can actually happen . . . almost all the board is under 40.
2003 New Mardi Gras Board Member

Many activists from the original homosexual rights vanguard defend an approach to queer liberation that is based on creating different ways and places of living and partying to the straight community. In contrast, younger activists from all over Australian are much more likely to be comfortable with a more integrated lifestyle than the older activists who congregate in inner cities. The Mardi Gras slogan 'Our Freedom, Your Freedom', says it all about this different approach.

Boomer gays were obsessed with 'the scene' because it offered them something extra to what they had, but today's gays don't even accept the label. They either don't want a label or don't define themselves through it. The activist contingent prefer 'queer' to 'gay' because it is more inclusive and a break from the restrictive past. For them equality is too generic and unfulfilling, and it's the young who have won the arguments and put their money where their mouth is with New Mardi Gras.

Where gay and lesbian activism once lagged behind other minority groups in terms of successes and structures, it now leads the way, thanks to its youthful dynamism. It's no surprise that most of the convenors of Australia's various queer/gay and lesbian rights bodies are aged roughly 30 or under. You could never say the same thing of ATSIC or women's organisations or unions. It's no surprise that the youth wing of all political parties have been outspoken in their opposition to discrimination against young gay and lesbian people. It's no surprise that the biggest queer conference in Australia is an annual student conference (Queer Collaborations). It's no surprise that more than half the people at the inaugural meeting of Rainbow Labor were young enough to be in Young Labor.

PLEASE JUST F* OFF . . . IT'S OUR TURN NOW

Legislation can't stop people from hating, but people can. Conscious acts at a personal, political and consumer level by millions of us have demonstrated our solidarity: by attending the Mardi Gras parade, by voting for queer people on *Big Brother* and by listening to their advice on sea-weed alpha-hydroxy moisturizer on *Queer Eye for the Straight Guy*. Those things move a community from a secure fringe to centre stage, and young people have supported that journey *en masse*.

Switching from particular communities to general innovation in methods there are several paths our activist communities simply must agree to follow.

Our activism should be about extending a hand to the inactive. Many people want to get involved in an issue, they want to have a conversation with power holders – but these people don't know where to start. Instead of shutting people out we need to let them in. NGOs, trade unions and political parties all need to develop better strategies for allowing systems of semi-formal membership to operate, for example. Many people will join an email list but not pay a membership fee, the important thing is keeping contact with them. You are giving them important information – distributing your key messages – at zero marginal cost if you do it through the Internet. No, we don't just want all these people floating around as information and resource sponges. No, we don't want flaky networks claiming to be serious political organisations. But there is a middle ground. Semi-formal membership is part of that ground and it cannot be dismissed as a halfway house or an option for wimps. It's not a free ride, it's a bridge to the disaffected.

It's sad that single issue or theme specific campaign groups can accept this while institutions like political parties do not. Addressing a small gathering of exiles in a restaurant overlooking London's Tower Bridge in June 2005, Carmen Lawrence made the graphic point that the US-based liberal campaign group **moveon.org** has more members and contributors in Australia (67,000 according to

Lawrence), than does the Australian Labor Party, even when you include it's paid-for stacked members! What more do you need to know?

Role model lobbying

In 2003 an unprecedented coalition of groups with a stake in a better education and training system came together to push a budget proposal on the Treasurer, Peter Costello. This is top-shelf Canberra lobbying, not fringe fence banging. We are talking the Business Council of Australia, the Australian Council of Social Services, the Australian Industry Group and the Australian Council of Trade Unions; not forgetting Jobs Australia, The Smith Family, the Dusseldorp Skills Forum, the Australian Council of State School Organisation and the Australian Secondary Principals' Association. Their pitch was called 'Boosting Young People's Educational and Economic Participation: Addressing the other end of the Inter-Generational Equation'.

In other countries with more competent and diverse media, this would receive attention and perhaps even a serious government response. In Australia it prompted neither. The heart of the proposal was the creation of 'a comprehensive National Youth Transition Service over five years.'[7] According to their pitch, getting at least 90 percent of young people actively participating in education, training and/or employment by 2009 has a benefit-to-cost ratio of at least 2.3:1. For an investment of just $240 million over six years – the price is barely worth mentioning. That's less than two dollars per person per year.

While there is a need to keep Baby Boomers participating in some capacity in the paid workforce after they turn 65, this is not the answer to our demographic challenge. Believing otherwise is simply placing Boomers at the centre of a debate – as the government does – that is mostly not about them. What we ought to do is follow the evidence of Access Economics and the advice of the Dusseldorp Skills Forum and the Business Council of Australia and invest more heavily in education and training for young people, changing the way they are taught and what they are taught at the same time. If we want to improve democracy, and we think having more well-educated young people is the way to go, that suggests some fundamental things – like teaching them about all the facets of our democracy in our education system and incorporating more democratic principles into that system. Once we've done that they might be able to use their new skills and knowledge to continue to desperately needed innovation in our workplaces.

Innovative workplaces

There are certain types of dynamic workplaces that are attractive to today's young 'career kangaroos'. Unions can decide whether they want to be a part of this dynamic movement, but, whether they do or not, the ideas are worth spreading. The starting point is to make our workplaces as socially inclusive as possible. In doing so we would be fitting into the core values of my generation but looking beyond our particular selfish interests.

> Hiring for diversity, once a matter of legal compliance, has become a matter of economic survival because creativity comes in all colours, genders and personal preferences.[8]

It's clear that you can make money out of being nice to all sorts of weird people, and the funny thing is that doing this makes them happier too. You can only do this by putting extra resources into merit-based recruiting and promotion and acting quickly on intelligence from talent-spotting initiatives. Diversity isn't just about race, gender, sexuality and religion though. We should also have the workplace maturity to systematically encourage:

- staff working from home
- staff having the option to buy extra annual leave
- providing fringe benefits like gym, child care and pool membership in salary packages, or free bicycles to employees to ride to work
- allowing flexible hours, rather than introducing capped hours
- tax deductible child care and paid parental leave.

These are the sorts of programs that Access Economics, in a 2005 study funded by the Australian Computer Society, are recommending. It would create 'a higher available talent pool, improved staff retention, productivity and higher quality of work'.[9] Having core business hours between 10 a.m. and 3 p.m. would allow people to work from 7 a.m. to 3 p.m. or 10 a.m. to 7 p.m., in accordance with their family needs, like dropping children off at school and picking them up. But these flexible systems must also understand that families don't usually have two kids and a picket fence. They could be a 21-year-old with a dog, a gay couple or Baby Boomer empty nesters. People move through life phases at different paces and in different directions. However annoying it might seem, our workplaces need to adapt to these facts or they will lose talent and money.

Cast your thoughts farther afield and imagine workplace snooze centres: the old school 'sick bay' from school crossed with a first class airline flatbed. Some will be aghast at the idea, but it already exists and we shouldn't be afraid to consider that plane of thinking. New Yorkers now have for-profit versions in their office blocks and they cost from $20 for 20 minutes – we could easily provide them free at the point of use in our workplaces.[10] From resting to exercising the opportunities retain the same magnetism.

According to a government study, obesity will become the leading cause of death in 2005 in the US – overtaking tobacco as the country's top killer. The answer to that problem isn't telling people to eat more vegetables it's giving them options and time for a healthier life. Can you think of a win:win result that unions could campaign for in this scenario?

In 2002 I floated the idea of free gym membership or vouchers for healthy lifestyle products and services being added to an ambit claim then being prepared by staff representatives negotiating for employees of ministers and parliamentarians. My argument was that a big wage claim would be a long, slow and mostly fruitless process while $1,500 worth of lifestyle vouchers would make each of us fitter, healthier and more relaxed. I was laughed out of town – when I wasn't being given a look normally reserved for the village idiot, that is. A year later we were still waiting for that pay rise. By comparison, the UK civil (public) service has no quibbles with interesting experiments. I currently ride a bike to work that was bought with a no-conditions interest free loan from work. And in general people like me who take up these offers take three days less sick leave a year. Don't whinge and churn out reports on obesity. Think laterally and act now.

Citizenship education

It sounds uninteresting but re-imagining citizenship must sit centre stage in my generation's strategy for change.

> WHEN we expect young people to want to know about social/political/world issues, they will become interested. Sometimes you need to demonstrate why an issue is important, and perhaps do a bit of extra work to present information in a way they can relate to – but they will be interested.
>
> *ABC journalist Angela Yeoh*[11]

Whether top rate incomes taxes are 48 cents or 45 cents in the dollar is nothing compared to whether a million kids are getting the information and hands-on experience they need to successfully navigate democracy in the 21st century.

Yet the most political people in our society – politicians – run like Cathy Freeman when it's suggested we need to teach 'political' ideas in our schools. You might as well suggest force-feeding Nazi propaganda to six-year-olds. We shouldn't 'politicise' children, apparently. What the hell does that even mean? In believing this nonsense we condemn future generations to disempowerment and marginalisation. Australia is shaping up to have an increasingly strong market coupled with an increasingly weak democracy. In the worst case scenario we will witness problems like young Muslims being marginalised out of their own communities by older leaders and left on the fringes of society in general. We should be asking ourselves what role proper, honest and universal citizenship education in our schools might play in stopping the next generation of terrorism. A few real discussions about what democracy is or could be are well worth the 'political' risk.

I vividly remember being taught as a four-year-old about the importance of money by a man from the Commonwealth Bank. Two years later I remember being indoctrinated to take my Catholic Confirmation and Holy Communion, not having a clue what either meant. But at no point do I remember learning anything about democracy other than that Tiananmen Square was bad and that the Senate has red seats.

Young people should learn about democracy in a universal, structured environment, and in our society that means schools. It's eminently sensible that they deliver comprehensive, relevant and meaningful citizenship education. The current pathetic placeholder in this respect is 'Discovering Democracy' – and it just will not do. It is essential that civics education content focuses on more than formal electoral politics, the constitution and the flag. Teaching on formal democratic institutions should be augmented with other material that reflects the fact that most things that change people's

PLEASE JUST F* OFF . . . IT'S OUR TURN NOW

lives happen outside Parliament. Most people don't want to be Natasha Stott-Despoja, but given half a chance they would probably be interested to learn how they can fix the things they see wrong in their community.

On that front, there is no better way to fix problems in communities than through the systemic support that could be offered by the reintroduction of national service into Australian life. Three, six or 12 months national service at the end of one's high school education is a very useful way to instil a public service ethos in the population while delivering practical benefits to people who need all kinds of help and support. In the 21st century I cannot think of anything more inappropriate than national service being thought of purely in military terms – service to the armed forces should be just one of many options available. The others should include work which is either character building or which would not otherwise be done – most obviously work in developing nations, and on projects providing aged care and environmental protection.

Without proper and sustained investment in civics and citizenship education we will continue to see a small, well-informed political oligarchy running pitched battles against the rest of society on issues crucial to everyone's future. Refugees and the republican referendum are key recent examples of this elitist trend. It's not sustainable to have a situation where people are literally scared off being involved in formal politics even when they want to be, or be fearful of admitting their political leanings because it might threaten their career or social standing.

> I had to make a decision a couple of years ago. DO I want to get involved in proper politics inside the party system or do I want to be involved in politics outside the system? I realised it would be a lot harder to achieve what I wanted if I was tainted by being in the system so I chose not to be.
>
> *Anonymous, 22*

Additionally we currently lack understanding of how individual decisions have collective consequences and what some of the links between them might be.

Growing good citizens is possible. Our step-by-step cultivation of young consumers is proof of the power of persistence. But as an increasingly diverse society it will become harder and harder to create a sense of shared citizenship.

Websites like **www.PolicyAtSchool.org** ('Dude, where's my rights?') and the Student Virtual Parliament should not have to fill the void on their own. It's the ultimate irony that governments have proven themselves incapable of advertising their own generic value. It's the responsibility of my generation to eliminate this credibility gap and educate a new generation to be informed participants in democracy. Then the quality of Australia's public conversation will improve.

For example, an OECD study argues that education is likely to be just as important as legislation (or even more so) in future attempts to protect the environment – the first of the 'glue issues' discussed in the next chapter. They believe good governance implies negotiation among informed partners, a process that requires well-educated, involved citizens. And you should be clear now that excellent citizenship education is essential.[12]

CHAPTER FOURTEEN

Glue issues

It's been two decades since the conservative US think tank industry devised the wedge issue strategy to split the US Democrats. Millions of us have cried recounting the number of column inches devoted to the 'wedge issues' dreamt up to keep the Howard Government installed on its throne. Yet where, in a decade, have you seen a single strategic solution for combating the 'wedge'? Enough of this tomfoolery! We need to identify 'glue issues' that bind us together. Defensively combating the issues most likely to tear us apart is the equivalent of fighting fire with fire. Let's start new ones instead.

What might a glue issue be? We would all agree that child abuse is a bad thing, but this isn't the foundation of a new Australia. An issue like the environment, however, is full of political capital. Almost everyone will tell you we should protect the environment – and that's half the battle won. There are many people for whom the ethical, spiritual or even sheer common sense case for protecting the environment is intuitive. They accept the need to change lifestyles and prioritise caring for the world around them.[1] Because the environment, like politics, is everywhere and affects all that we do to some extent, the two are perfect for mingling.

The challenge of a glue issue is turning that abstract acknowledgement into passionate belief, concrete action, or a vote. Glue issues are more than triangulation; they are a set of political values that search out and prime up the best human instincts.[2] Glue issues encourage people to be secure and generous enough to put themselves second to a greater good.

If we can adopt and deliver on glue issues we can prove ourselves to be mature and responsible, as I've claimed. Three examples of possible glue issues are the environment, childhood development and affordable housing. Each is compelling, each could be popular and each needs skilled advocates. Of course these issues have had active campaigners for decades, and even centuries. My particular contribution is to demand these issues be viewed with a new, different and specific political potential as glue issues. The challenge is to make these issues and viewpoints the ones you simply cannot disagree with in the 21st century.

The environment

First things first. What do we want to achieve and why? I ask the question not to elicit an exact answer but to emphasise that we have choices when it comes to the environment. Just as our consumer experience reminds us of the primacy of choice in our life, so should the future of our natural environment. We have choices about what happens to it and the choice should be in the interest of the common wealth, rather than choosing to dig it up, burn it up or otherwise waste it. To deny concepts like climate change is to mark yourself out as a standard bearer of an aggressive depravity that borders on the criminal. The science academies of the G8 nations and those of China, India and Brazil all acknowledge the threat posed by climate change. The president of the world's oldest scientific organisation, the Royal Society, dismisses any suggestion of there even being a debate about climate change. If there even is a debate it is, he says, 'like Manchester United taking on three schoolchildren.'[3] In Australia eminent scientists like Tim Flannery warn of the drying out of Eastern Australia. That is, you're not witnessing 'droughts' on TV anymore – because they aren't 'droughts', they're the norm. The latest international polling (conducted in mid 2005) finds that 90 percent of Westerners believe 'the effects of climate change are becoming increasingly apparent', and 79 percent think humans are 'primarily responsible'.[4] The response of the US, China and Australia – the Asia-Pacific Partnership on Clean Development and Climate – shows once and for all that the reality climate change is undeniable, even if the framework of the Kyoto Protocol is.

So we see opinion on the side of the environment and we see the powerful increasingly willing to back it. John Howard and other senior Liberals agree it's a mainstream issue, all this just 20 years after Chernobyl and the UN's Brundtland Report which popularised sustainability.[5] And if nothing else, sustainability is inseparable from intergenerational equity.[6]

So why has the ALP's only legacy from the Franklin Dam campaign been a clumsy last minute conversion to the plight of old growth forests in Tasmania? Any student or earth mother can offer you that – it's hardly a deal maker from an opposition leader. The same goes for signing for Kyoto protocol. Just because it takes a Herculean effort to convince your party room colleagues that the environment is an investment and a vote winner, it doesn't mean people at home in their kitchen cabinets are going to give you a pat on the back. It has the same impact of a motel advertising that is has colour TV. The reaction is 'well, duh!, of course'. There are just some things you are meant to do if you're a good opposition or government. Caring about the environment is now one of them.

Political parties should offer radical (and they will often be expensive at face value) environmental policies to prove their commitment. And we should all remember that alongside greater investment in all levels of education, the environment is the most tangible issue with which to demonstrate a commitment to intergenerational equity.

The buck starts here and potential needs to translate into cash and action now. We need, for instance, to prove that sustainability can boost corporate performance. Right now the companies most affected by the environment are the ones wrecking it and making fortunes. Check out Al Gore's Generation Investment Management firm (www.generationim.com) for a sample of someone dedicated to the case. We have to radically overhaul the role of agriculture in our society and economy and we must establish systems that enforce correct pricing – making companies and governments incorporate the environmental costs of their business models in their accounts. It's what *The Economist* likes to think of as the mating of Rachel Carson and Adam Smith. Need an example? Don't ban cars – use new fuels like ethanol to power them. Nothing could be more This Generation than that.

Affordable housing

Affordable housing is the new superannuation. Just as superannuation will save millions from downgraded lifestyles or outright poverty as they age, an affordable housing movement has the potential to do the same. And if we don't find a way to achieve this, terms like 'property apartheid' will be 100 percent serious rather than a bitter personal interpretation of the property market.

Perhaps even ahead of health care and behind only food, housing is the most basic human requirement. Yet negative gearing and other tax breaks resemble out of control private health insurance subsidies more than they resemble Medicare. Affordable housing is structurally discouraged by negative gearing tax policies. Why would anyone invest in budget housing if they had a choice? It's a recipe for lower returns – so they don't. I don't want to stop people investing in the property market but there should be incentives to invest in affordable housing. There are a limited number of properties and I want to make sure they are not concentrated at three properties a pop amongst the 55-year-olds of the country.

If Australians can love and cherish Medicare they can love and cherish public and affordable housing too. It just doesn't suit the dinner party commentariat to make the sustained arguments to enforce these policies. We need to mandate proportions of affordable housing; it should be part of the 21st century social contract.

Currently, investors sink their cash into properties that most can barely afford – driving up rents and creating an imbalance in the market that is difficult to correct. Investors get huge tax deductions and as they can leverage off their existing property assets they avoid the relatively huge deposit burden that the young face and must scrape together. Assuming that no government is going to abolish negative gearing in the near future, this unfair advantage should be balanced out by first home buyers being allowed to claim back some of their interest payments as a tax deduction, or another similar innovation. This would be far better than inflationary policies like the First Home Owners Grant.

An additional approach may be to place restrictions on purchase of second and third homes. Banning these purchases is impractical and the losers from such a system are rich enough to cause grief to any government brave enough to try. But forcing these third home owners to offer 20 or 30 percent of the capital in that property to a young person as a condition of sale is a workable idea that does not depend on a generous or able family stepping into this breach. Just as we have waiting lists for Housing Commission properties now we can have a young person's register from which individuals could be matched with older property purchasers and given the opportunity to build up their asset base.

Superannuation funds are another obvious pressure point for more affordable housing. More than $500 billion is currently invested in Australia's superannuation funds – 80 percent of it in

Australia. There are 109 industry funds in Australia where union representatives make up 50 percent of the board. With the support of just another 10 percent of board members you have access to the capital needed to drive an affordable housing revolution in Australia. The 78 public-sector (government employee) funds have at least three million members and more than $100 billion in assets – that's another very big springboard for action.

There's absolutely no reason why a 21st century Commonwealth Bank cannot be established in order to improve access to the property market for young people and, indeed, all renters. If any government were brave enough to abolish negative gearing the savings could be used to fund such an agency. Institutions structured to focus on home loans already exist – they can even afford to have stadiums named after themselves they have been so popular. You can bet that if it was deemed politically imperative the Americans would find a way to do it. Oh, that's right . . . they already have a federal mortgage bank.

London's Mayor, Ken Livingstone has a policy that 50 percent of new homes be 'affordable', while the UK national government is overseeing the construction of two million new homes by 2010. Can you imagine the equivalent in Australia – 600,000 new homes by 2010? It's my generation's job to make this the new Australian dream.

The government spends more than a billion dollars a year on rent assistance – but it's simply a wealth transfer to rich landlords. The rent assistance money is transferred into higher rental rates. Like the First Home Owners Grant it doesn't expand access to the property market – it just inflates prices. As such, rent assistance should be phased out over the course of a decade and the money transferred to public housing. You couldn't do it straight away because you need to build up the stock of public housing.

This investment in public housing will need to happen soon – it is now reasonably popular to suppose that public housing won't survive another decade. The problem, according to the Australian Housing and Urban Research Institute, is that the various public housing bodies are all running unsustainable deficits. So what about a levy to fund the deficits of public housing bodies? If you are going to push property prices by investing in yet another expensive development then it's only fair you put a bit back in to help glue all the broken bits of society back together.

However, it's the field of design where we see issues like housing and the environment combine with innovation to hit the policy stratosphere. Our local councils do not support risk and innovation in design. New forms of architecture are treated as a threat rather than an opportunity, an overdevelopment until proven otherwise. Councils just think they have a licence to blandify design rather than do anything useful like promote social equity. This needn't be the case.

Increased direct investment in public housing would enlarge the market for sustainable housing materials, making them cheaper and bringing down rents in the process by expanding the rental market. Sustainable housing is also likely to be medium or high density housing – a very useful lesson for all current and prospective home buyers. According researchers from the Globalisation and World Cities study group 'cities will be essential for saving nature'.[7] High-density housing can easily equal good quality of life. Look at the standard of living in our new inner cities compared to that of the average middle ring suburb or country town. Look at the education levels, incomes and mobility of those who live in inner cities – these are wealthier, healthier places all round. With this understanding out goes the argument that you need a quarter-acre block and all the social inertia, wasted roads and pointless infrastructure that goes with them to have a decent domestic life.

Residential housing of the future needs to be based around higher densities, better use of space, diversity in design and internal flexibility.[8] We know we'll have done well when people can easily refit their houses to accommodate major changes like the birth of children. Which brings us to our third glue issue – childhood development.

Childhood development

If you don't invest in childcare and education the state has to pay later anyway – supporting welfare for single parents, paying for underperforming children, coping with an underperforming labour force.

The Blair Government is extending non-compulsory school hours to 5 p.m. and sometimes 6 p.m., with learning and extra-curricula activities in preference to the lost hours that are after-school care. This is a big win for working parents who can't nick off from work at 2.30 p.m. every single day. It means fancy activities for all kids – not just the pampered denizens of the private system. Australian governments ought to recognise the amazing capital, culture and community hub sitting in the grounds of their schools. These places are more than a hall to be rented to local craft fairs. They are the new roots of new communities that could sustain themselves for generations to come if designed correctly and in the right spirit.

How can we re-introduce to public life the ethic of wanting a better world for the generations after us? That's the key question. Promoting childhood development as a glue issue is a way for our generation to assert up front, right now, that we don't want to have a good time at the expense of those that follow.

It's the humane thing to do and it is the efficient thing to do. 'The data, without exception, speak to the impact of early care and education on early learning, high-school graduation, and even on later home-ownership among participants.'[9] One US pre-school development programme that has been operating since the 1960s has recently demonstrated a return of $17 of for every $1 spent on it. You can't get more explicit proof of value than that.[10] And for the grand package of universal pre-school, Swedish family-leave policies and French childcare provisions, it would probably cost less than two percent of gross domestic product.[11]

A colleague of mine puts it like this:

> Boomers are sucking the blood out of Xers. We work like dogs, pay hideous rents, have no job security, and are so exhausted we have no time any more to think, let alone raise questions about the status quo and take action. Boomers aren't interested in us, except as a source of tax revenue for their pensions and looming health-care costs. That's why they're freaked that we're not having babies.

If we're serious about sticking with capitalism and making it better then we also need urgently to tackle the dysfunctional relationship the free market has with innocent children. Just look at the increasing number of overweight children pumped full of sugar, fat and other crap by ruthless food producers, marketers and parents who couldn't say no. This is a perfect example of where a free market helps no one. The plight of these children is attracting serious medical attention across the West. 'Obesity is the consequence of a revolution in diet and lifestyle that has occurred over the past 25 years. We have access to cheap, energy-dense food but, critically, we exercise less.'[12] It leaves society with a big expensive government (the health costs) and unhappy people (the junk food leaving you sluggish and with body image issues). And excluding easy targets like McDonalds – who are finally learning the lesson that it's bad to make toxic dumps out of your customer's bodies – we have a food industry that is in denial about it all. It is the tobacco industry of the 21st century and the problem isn't going away.

The obvious place to start is to ban junk food advertising aimed at kids or screened during children's TV programs. Apparently the advertisers and the channels can see this coming, even if the government can't. That's why they're meeting to offer up some morsels to create a veneer of caring about healthy lifestyles. The clearly vacuous Australian Association of National Advertisers says: 'We're exploring a range of options that could lead to one or more initiatives that further use the resources of the advertising and media sectors.'[13] They should stop exploring and start doing, and from our politicians to our parents the rest of us can join them at it.

But as any half-fit person knows, it's exercise not just diet that delivers you a functioning body. That means grassroots sports as well as major sporting events need subsidies. Parents need to be fitness role models and they should be supported by their workplaces to be those role models – that's where innovation in the work/life balance debate can contribute to childhood development.

You'd have to be a bastard not to want to invest in children, so let's show what an unbastardly cohort Australians are and ramp up the investment.

Conclusion

This book is not the answer to generational inequity – you are. Whether you are one of my age peers or one of those I've tried to hold to account – you are capable of being part of making a better Australia. It's the spirit of possibility that Claudia O'Keefe, the 2004 *Economist* essay winner, encapsulates when she writes:

> ... once we agree the past cannot be recaptured, we will at last open ourselves to solutions we haven't yet considered ... only when we accept the future that awaits us can we embrace a more thrilling successor to outmoded twentieth-century ideals.[1]

Let us stop underselling ourselves. Let's be optimistic and show hope. Optimism for what Australia is capable of, and hope that things will get better if young and innovative people are allowed to get on with the job and take charge of the job.

Making generational change happen is difficult. Sweeping aside mediocrity as we do it will be even harder, but it will be fun. I wish we could just wave a wand and march into action, but each of our niches in government, activism, corporate life, the media, or suburbia

CONCLUSION

is not enough on its own. The reality is, you can't drive complex change from the centre – you have to drive it everywhere. It helps to have leaders and institutions on the side of change, but if we indulge ourselves in the belief that a new young elite can control or own a movement for renewal then we will be repeating the very mistakes of the Baby Boomer elite I criticise.

We must also accept the contradictory truth that many actual solutions will be simple. They must be simple because in world of mind-boggling choices only cold, hard excellent simplicity will stand out enough to cut through and achieve change at the scale I suggest we need.

And we must persist even when things look grim. New ideas and systems always endure grim moments, but that's where my generation's capacity for innovation and risk-taking comes in. Innovation is not about the easy option; it's not about bailing out when things get tough. As the responsible generation we can take these risks with a firm insurance – the knowledge that we will stick by the tough decisions.

Let's not defer to the nay-sayers. Let's take all our talents, communication skills and technology savvy and give society a heart starter like it hasn't had since . . . no I'm not going to mention the past. It's about us. Let's sing the praises of our diversity, our relationships and our communities and put them up as role models for the rest. And let's acknowledge that someone else will do it better one day and that we want to help them get there.

Fiona Stewart of www.notgoodenough.org is right – there are many things in Australia that 'aren't fucking good enough'.[2] And we've a right to say so and to do it on a media platform. Many and perhaps most of the millions who have left Australia want to come back – that's evidence that it's worth fighting for a different Australia. The only way to do that in an orderly fashion is to fight the Boomers and work with them at the same time.[3] Mere fighting can't deliver glue issues, and subservient cooperation can't produce innovation, and we need it all.

When I think back again to Gallipoli or our World War II veterans I'm reminded that they did not fight and die for Boomers to faff around worrying about unobscured water views, orgasm over Plasma TV, wear designer jeans and attend rock concerts well after qualifying for a Seniors Card. No, that's not what these people suffered for; it's not what my generation want to turn into; and it is not what will make Australia great in the 21st century. Making Australia a society of excellence and compassion makes their sacrifice worthwhile. Fostering that spirit of innovation and entrepreneurialism and social solidarity will bring its own rewards. It is only my generation that can deliver all that.

The case for investing in youth is self-evident. Whether it is open minds, fertility or sheer zest for life, the young have the most potential to deliver for us all. Making that effort requires less a leap of faith than a leap of imagination. The question is whether Australians are up to the task.

When I think of Australia at its best, it is unbeatable. Australia at its best searches the world for inspiration and cherry-picks the most interesting, efficient and pragmatic ways forward. We have closed up before – between the wars, and again in the 1950s and '60s – and we got over it. We need to look outward again. We can be either a dynamic society or a passive society, insular or open. We can learn to change or we can learn nothing and be conservative. We can take risks and manage them or we can act like children afraid of the dark. This is not the same as recreating life under the Hawke–Keating government but it's about recapturing a reforming zeal and applying it better and in more relevant ways to the lives and choices of 21st-century Australia.

Let's not wallow in the easy option of yet another mind-numbing talk fest or a corporate sponsored festival of ideas that really contain no ideas at all because they contain only the same ideas you've heard

CONCLUSION

How will we know things have changed?

1. Every major ASX listed company will have executives in charge of corporate social responsibilities and reputation, signalling a wider cultural change.
2. We will have levelled off, and possibly dragged down the human capital flight from Australia.
3. A reformed HECS system will not be a deterrent to study nor a block on greater public investment in tertiary education.
4. There will be a string of Cabinets where women and people from ethnic, racial and sexual minorities aren't the odd ones out.
5. Conservative religion will remain one of many competing faiths and philosophies, and not a major force in either electoral politics or public policy formation.
6. Information technologies will be seen as the vital public utilities they are, and our media will be competitive and diverse not flaccid, boring and old.
7. Superannuated Boomers will take responsibility for themselves in an embrace of mutual obligation which recognises *we* are footing the rest of the bill.
8. Innovation and entrepreneurialism will be understood as concepts covering more than technology and economic productivity: they will be bywords for our national ideals.
9. Glue issues like the environment, early childhood investment and affordable housing will have been pushed into the centre of politics.
10. A new book like this one will not be necessary in ten years, because the messages have hit home.
11. My generation will exit the stage gracefully in recognition that our successors can do it better.

before. Let's not wallow in an old economy of dwindling exports, mounting debt and a flawed property market when we can have an economy run on skills, good ideas and an entrepreneurial spirit.

Light at the end of the tunnel

Sophocles, the Greek dramatist (considered by Aristotle to be an innovator), wrote: 'sometimes you have to wait until the evening to see how glorious the day has been.' It will be sad if we do have to wait decades to lose our collective humility and shyness – there is much about my generation to be appreciated right now, while we still have the energy to do it. We need to push ourselves forward so society may be pulled along with us.

In 1997 *The Australian*, in its Editorial no less, announced our 'failure – relative to the '70s generation – to swing the cultural high wire with anything like the panache of the boomers'.[4] That's nonsense and you know it.

And if we don't succeed at every turn and with every new idea, we need to be able to say we tried to the change the place. You will be proud if you can sit back at 50 and say to yourself: I tried, at least I did that.

Endnotes

Introduction

1 Ken Henry, quoted by Matt Wade in 'Don't worry, be wealthy', *Sydney Morning Herald*, 18 May 2005.
2 'Ten ways to change the world', <http://www.annesummers.com.au/actingup.htm> [viewed 12 July 2005].
3 Mark Henderson, *The Times* (UK), 13 November 2004.
4 Damian Barr, 'Young Britain – nation of selves, not necessarily selfish', *The Times*, September 13, 2004.
5 Peter Duncan, 'Corporate Social Responsibility – A Shell view', summary of a speech of the same title to the Sydney Institute, 29 March 2000, as published in *The Sydney Papers*, Autumn 2000.
6 Scott Carn, interview, May 2004.

Chapter One

1 Paul McCartney, at the opening of an exhibition of photos of his latest world tour – called *Each One Believing*, Pendennis column, *The Observer* (UK), 7 November 2004.
2 Mary O'Hara, 'Talkin' bout your generation', *The Observer* (UK), 22 March 2004.
3 Daniel Dasey, 'Age is just a number – 5000', *The Sun-Herald*, 26 December 2004.

4 Sarah Boseley, 'More sex please – we're young, female and liberated', Society section, *The Guardian*, 30 November 2001.
5 Daniel Donahoo, 'Why Mum and Dad's became Peter Pan's never-ever land', Comment section, *Sydney Morning Herald*, 27 December 2004.
6 Richard Florida, *The Rise of the Creative Class*, Pluto Press, Sydney, 2003, p. 10.
7 'The Bridget Jones economy', *The Economist*, from *The Economist* print edition 20 December 2001 [viewed at www.economist.com/diversion/printerFriendly.cfm?Story_ID=883664 on 14 August 2005].
8 Lenny Ann Low, 'From the other side of the youth divide, it's not nearly as wide as it looked', *Sydney Morning Herald*, 30 January 2005.
9 Alan Mascarenhas and Justin Norrie, 'Older doctors suffer the shock of the new', *Sydney Morning Herald*, 16 February 2005, quoting Harvard Medical School research where 45 of 59 studies linked age of years since graduation with inferior knowledge, resistance to new better techniques and other problems; 'Seniors need more of a brain than young people', *Senior Journal*, 17 August 2001.
10 David Dale, quoting Measures of Social Progress 2004 (ABS) in 'More healthy, more wealthy: a year of living easier', *Sydney Morning Herald*, 27 December 2004, p. 6.
11 'Brains Of Those In Certain Professions Shown To Have More Synapses,' Science Daily, 3 December 1999, http://biology.about.com/gi/dynamic/offsite.htm?site=http://www.sciencedaily.com/releases/1999/12/991203081719.htm [viewed 5 July 2005].
12 Sarah Baxter, 'Couch potatoes sprout bigger brains watching TV', *The Sunday Times* (UK), 1 May 2005.
13 Madeleine Bunting, *The Guardian*, 13 Nov 2000.
14 'The art of work and the work of art in the 21st century', www.richardneville.com.au [viewed 14 August 2005].
15 Damian Barr, 'Young Britain – nation of selves, not necessarily selfish', *The Times*, 13 September 2004.
16 *Sydney Morning Herald*, 18 February 2005.
17 Results of an OMM (Observer Music Magazine) poll as published by Sean O'Hagan in 'Why Lennon Lives On,' *The Observer*, 14 August 2005, p. 1 of Review section.
18 *The Australian Way* [Qantas domestic and international in-flight magazine], December 2004, p. 245.
19 Paul McCartney's estimated worth as published in Adam Sherwin's

'Rock legends of the Sixties turn back the clock – in their sixties,' *The Times*, 8 August 2005, p. 5.
20 Adam Sherwin's 'Rock legends of the Sixties turn back the clock – in their sixties,' *The Times*, 8 August 2005, p. 5.
21 Andere Paine, 'Worth every penny: 2500 pounds a second Macca bowls the US over', *Evening Standard* (London), 7 February 2005.
22 Tim Watts, Hugh Martin and Fiona Stewart, *The Age* Opinion section, 29 Jan 2002.
23 Narayana Murthy, 'Globalcorp 2005', in *The Economist*'s 'The World in 2005' report, *The Economist*, December 2004, p. 114.
24 Survey of 100 young people undertaken by Vibewire, www.vibewire.net [viewed May 2005].
25 Ben Wyld, 'The Reason Y', 10 August 2005, http://radar.smh.com.au/archives/2005/08/companies_are_e.html
26 Guardian ICM poll (UK), December 2004.
27 Alice Thomson, 'Pop Idol wins over politicians', *The Daily Telegraph*, 7 March 2005.

Chapter Two

1 'Growing into Giving', survey by the UK Charities Aid Foundation, 2002.
2 Danielle Teutsch, 'Boomers lack benevolence', *Sun-Herald*, 7 December 2003.
3 Todd Gitlin, *Letters to a Young Activist*, Basic Book, Cambridge MA., 2003.
4 Tactical Response Police numbering more than 100 were brought into North Sydney and evacuated the entire North Sydney CBD. The police later apologised in person the group who had been arrested when we were gathered in a room at North Sydney police station after police interviews had been conducted. We were then released from custody.
5 'Stink Plan to quell protests', *The Australian*, IT Today section (originally published in *The Economist*), 21 December 2004.
6 From www.theoaktree.org [viewed 19 June 2005].
7 Michael Ostrolenk, 'Beyond Left and Right: Toward A New Transpartisan Politics', www.freeliberal.com/arhicves/000197.html [viewed 15 August 2005].
8 Roberto Unger quoted by James Crabtree, July 2005, in an interview unpublished at the time of writing.

Chapter Three

1 *The Observer*, 3 April 2005.
2 Quoted by Guy Kawasaki in *Rules for Revolutionaries*, HarperBusiness, 1999, New York, p. 164.
3 David Smith, '2050 – and immortality is within our grasp', *The Observer* (UK), 22 May 2005.
4 Jayne Atherton, 'The disposable 16-pound camcorder', *Metro* (London), 7 June 2005.
5 Guy Kawasaki, *Rules for Revolutionaries*, pp. 70–71.
6 Leo Lewis, 'Old technophobes find it's easy to talk on the foolproof mobile', *The Times*, 17 February 2005.
7 Tim Duggan, 23, Sydney, interview by email,1 June 2004.
8 Tim Duggan, 23, Sydney, interview by email, 1 June 2004.
9 Carly Fiorina, 'Totally Digital', *The Economist*'s *'The World in 2005'*, 2004, p. 128.
10 Simon Waldman, 'Coming to a hard disk near you', *Guardian*, G2 supplement, 17 June 2005.
11 Deidre Macken, 'Check your pulse: the future arrives faster these days', *The Australian Financial Review*, Perspective section, 29 December 2004.
12 Howard Rheingold, *Smart Mobs: The Next Social Revolution*, Perseus, Cambridge MA, pp. 15–25.
13 Rheingold, *Smart Mobs*, pp. 15–25.
14 David Rowan, 'World in Auction', *The Sunday Times Magazine* (UK), 20 February 2005.
15 Rheingold, *Smart Mobs*, pp. 93–112.
16 'All the news that's fit to blog', Simon Waldman (director of digital publishing at Guardian Newspapers), *The Guardian Review*, 6 November 2004.
17 Tom Morton, 'Uncle Sam's bastard children', *Griffith Review*, Autumn 2004, p. 181.
18 Posting to 'lateboomers@yahoogroups.com', 2.52 p.m. 31 March 2004.
19 Andrew Losowsky, 'A 21st-century protest' www.mediaguardian.co.uk [25 Mar. 2004].

Chapter Four

1 Eamonn Kelly and Peter Leyden (eds.), *What's Next: Exploring the New Terrain for Business*, Perseus Publishing, Cambridge MA, 2002, p. 2.
2 Kelly and Leyden, *What's Next*, p. 3.

3 Chris Chesher, 'Connection unbound by location', *Griffith Review*, Autumn 2004, p. 192.
4 Danielle Teutsch, 'Warning signs can be subtle', *Sun-Herald*, 6 June 2004.
5 Simon Castles quoting the American psychologist Jean Twenge in his article 'The Suicide Generation', *The Age*, 23 November 2004.
6 Kerryn Goldsworthy, *Australian Book Review*, May 2001 (reviewing *Other People's Words* by Hilary McPhee).
7 Abby Wilner, 'The age of discontent', *Sydney Morning Herald*, Radar section, 10 March 2004.
8 'Loyalty and Flexibility', *The HR Director's Yearbook 2005*, Keeping People section, Haymarket Publishing, London, January 2005.
9 British career management consultants Penna Saunders and Sidney, December 2003.
10 Simon Caulkin, 'How to catch a rising star', *The Observer* (UK), 9 November 2003.
11 Richard Reeves, 'The young ones', Work Unlimited, *The Guardian* (UK), 3 Jan. 2001.

Chapter Five

1 Suzy Austin, '211m children work as slaves, warns U.N.', *Metro* (London), 21 February 2005.
2 Jemima Lewis, 'Since when did work bring you happiness', *The Independent*, Opinion section, 1 August 2005, p. 31.
3 'The facts about flying', *The Independent* (UK), 28 May 2005.
4 Adapted from calculations in 'Why that cheap flight carries a huge cost for the environment', *The Independent* (UK), 28 May 2005.
5 Decca Aitkenhead, 'Apathy in the U.K.', *The Guardian*, 29 April 2002.
6 'Sniffer does bust 120 for drugs', *Sydney Morning Herald*, 26 January 2005.

Chapter Six

1 George Quinn (head of the Southeast Asia Centre at the Australian National University), *Canberra Times*, 12 February 2004.
2 Robert Miliken, 'Still feeling lucky?', in *The Economist*'s *The World in 2005* edition, 2004, p. 80.

3 Tony Moore, 'These babies stopped booming in 1975', *The Australian*, 20 February 1997.
4 Ruth Gamble, Letter to the Editor, *Sunday Age*, 17 April 1994, as quoted in Mark Davis, *Gangland – Cultural Elites and the New Generationalism*, Allen and Unwin, 1997, p. 3.
5 Bernard Salt, 'The Great Showdown', *Sydney Morning Herald*, Spectrum section, 20 September 2003.
6 Miranda Devine, 'The boom and bust of generation wars', *Sydney Morning Herald*, 12 May 2005.
7 Tony Moore, 'Pity the poor boomers, hanging on for dear life', *Sydney Morning Herald*, January 2002.
8 Stephen Alomes, 'Cultural Radicalism in the Sixties', *Arena*, 1983 (supplied from the research files of Tony Moore), pp. 29–30.
9 Gregg Flynn, *The Australian*, 5 April 1995.
10 Alomes, 'Cultural Radicalism in the Sixties', p. 34.
11 Pam Woodall, 'Home truths', p. 133.
12 Pam Woodall, 'Home truths', p. 133; JP Morgan estimate quoted in an editorial of the *Sydney Morning Herald*, 'The auction that had to end', *Sydney Morning Herald*, August 13, 2005.
13 Generation Xcluded, *Sunday Age*, 21 December 2003.
14 Raymond Bonner, 'Hole in the housing bubble', *New York Times*, 5 July 2005.
15 'A survey of Australia', *The Economist*, 7 May 2005, p. 7.
16 Dominic Knight, 'It's the Folks' Fault the Kids Can't Move Out', *Sydney Morning Herald*, Comment section, 24 March 2004.
17 Mark Schifter, 'Calling all young dentists – we need just two years of your time', *Sydney Morning Herald*, Opinion section, 16 February 2005.
18 Raymond Bonner, 'Hole in the housing bubble'.
19 Mora Main, Letter to the Editor, *Sydney Morning Herald*, 23 December 2004.
20 *Sydney Morning Herald* reporting on Ian MacFarlane's 18 February 2005 statement about interest rates.
21 Matt Wade and John Garnaut, 'The Goldilocks years are over', *Sydney Morning Herald*, 19 February 2005.
22 David Penberthy, 'Payback politics – bet your house on it', *Daily Telegraph*, 7 April 2004.
23 Anne Davies, 'Hopes rise for investment property tax change', *Sydney Morning Herald*, 16 February 2005.
24 Anne Davies, 'Hopes rise for investment property tax change'.

25 Michael Evans and Lisa Pryor, 'Outrage as Egan bites both ends of the sale', *Sydney Morning Herald*, 7 April 2004.
26 Adele Horin, 'Punted on land and lost? Tough', *Sydney Morning Herald*, Opinion section, 13 August 2005.

Chapter Seven

1 *Times Higher Education Supplement* (UK), 2003.
2 Adele Horin, 'Ailing unis are the great class levellers', *Sydney Morning Herald*, 13 May 2005.
3 Quotes in Depra Jopson and Kelly Burke, 'Red ink, ivory towers', *Sydney Morning Herald*, 13 May 2005.
4 Aban Contractor, 'Students expelled for working in sex industry', *Sydney Morning Herald*, 27 December 2004.
5 From Alison Pressley, *Living in the '70s*, Random House, Sydney, 1998, various pages.
6 Claim made by the 2003 National Union of Students President Daniel Kyriacou when interviewed by me in April 2004.
7 Mark Davis, 'Great White Noise', *Sydney Morning Herald*, 11 November 2002.
8 Johann Hari, 'I have seen the future and it's lousy', *New Statesman*, 5 February 2001.
9 Access Economics Report for the Dusseldorp Skills Forum and Business Council of Australia, *The Economic Benefit of Increased Participation in Education and Training*, Dusseldorp Skills Forum, Glebe, June 2005, p. 8.

Chapter Eight

1 Peter Duncan, Chairman and Chief Executive Officer of Shell Australia, in his speech to The Sydney Institute, 'Corporate Social Responsibility – a Shell view', 29 March 2000, in *The Sydney Papers*, Autumn 2000.
2 Bill Clinton, *My Life*, Arrow Books, Random House, UK, 2005, p. 185.
3 Simon Longstaff, 'Excess baggage', *Sydney Morning Herald*, 28 August 2002.
4 Ernst and Young '*Corporate Governance Update*', general newsletter published by Ernst and Young, April 2004.
5 Fred Hilmer, transcript of his speech to The Sydney Institute 'The

politics of media regulation', in *The Sydney Papers*, Summer 2000, p. 47.
6   Charles Handy, 'Democracy's new frontier', *The Economist*'s *The World in 2005*, 2004, p. 124.
7   Andrew Cornell, 'Happy Christmas, Bankers', *Australian Financial Review*, Perspective section, 23–28 December 2004.
8   '"Shameful" pay makes British women worst of in Europe', Jamie Doward and Tom Reilly, *The Observer* (UK), 12 October 2003.
9   Paul Hawken in Kelly and Leyden, *What's Next*, p. 260.
10 ww.goodcorporation.com [viewed 9 August 2005].
11 Katherine Fulton in Kelly and Leyden, *What's Next*, p. 287.
12 'Face value: Lord of the rings', *The Economist*, 5 February 2005, p. 66.
13 Katherine Fulton in Kelly and Leyden, *What's Next* p. 288.
14 Definition given by Skoll Foundation http://www.sbs.ox.ac.uk/downloads/skollfactsheet.pdf [viewed 9 August 2005].
15 From the Said Business School website, Oxford University, http://www.sbs.ox.ac.uk/html/faculty_skoll_about.asp [viewed 9 August 2005].

Chapter Nine

1   Another delight from the short-lived *Strewth* magazine.
2   Rob Johnson, speech to The Sydney Institute, 'Critic Critique Thyself: the media and self-delusion', 8 May 2001, as published in *The Sydney Papers*, Winter 2001.
3   According David Sifry on blog tracking site Technorati, <www.technorati.com/weblog/>, 'state of the Blogosphere', August 2005, Part 2: Posting Volume, and Part 1: Blog Growth.
4   According to *The Guardian*'s 2005 Media Power list, http://media.guardian.co.uk/top100_2005/index/0,16108,1513913,00.html viewed 18 July 2005.
5   A creator led scheme in which authors of artistic work are encouraged to give up some of their rights to the 'commons.' The movement is generally considered to be led by Professor Lawrence Lessig of Stanford University Law School and unofficially operates under the slogan 'some rights reserved.'
6   Based on a range of sources from metropolitan media outlets and political parties.
7   Megan Elliot, 1 Sept 2004 <http://www.newmatilda.com/home/articledetail.asp?ArticleID=73> [viewed 30 August 2005].
8   Stephen Mayne, 'The appalling culture of The Daily Telegraph,' www.

crikey.com.au, 1 September 2005.

9   Julianne Schultz, New Matilda, posted at http://www.newmatilda.com/home/articledetail.asp?ArticleID=285 20 October 2004, [viewed 30 August 2005].

10 Andrew Marr quoting Phillip Knightley in *My Trade: a short history of British Journalism*' Pan Books, London, 2004, pp. 89–90

11 Analogy adapted from Jesse Sunenblick, 'Into the Great Wide Open', *Columbia Journalism Review*, 2005, http://www.cjr.org/issues/2005/2/sunenblick.asp

12 Dawn Airey, Managing Director of Sky Networks UK, describing the era prior to the '400 channel universe', *The Independent*, 'Media Weekly' supplement,1 August 2005, p. 10.

13 *Young People and Media: Opposite Sides of the Fence? An account of young people's attitudes towards, experiences of, portrayals by and assumptions about media in Australia*, compiled by Simon Moss, Dee Jefferson and Dinah Arndt, September 2004, p. 23.

14 Lawrence Wilkinson, producer and co-founder of Oxygen Media, in Kelly and Leyden, *What's Next*, p. 176.

15 'Right on capitalism', Thereader.com.au, edition 60, August 2004.

16 Referring to Brian Henderson in Sydney and Brian Naylor in Melbourne.

17 Moss, Jefferson and Arndt, *Young People and Media: Opposite Sides of the Fence?*, pp. 72–94.

18 More4 advertising booklet, London, 9 October 2005

19 Geoff Kitney, 'U.K.'s digital TV revolution has lessons for Australia', *Australian Financial Review*, Perspective section, 23–28 December 2004.

20 Mark Kleinman, 'Union attacks BBC over sale to Australian bank,' Business section, *Sunday Times* (UK), 3 July 2005.

21 Alexia Baracaia, 'Rap for the BBC digital shows "no one watches"', *Evening Standard*, 13 October 2004.

22 Tony Moore, 'Managers are stifling our creativity,' *Sydney Morning Herald*, Opinion section, 6 April 2004.

23 Tony Moore, 'Unchaining the ABC', in Dennis Glover and Glenn Patmore (eds.) *For the People: Labor Essays 2000–2001*, Pluto Press, Annandale, 2001, p. 98.

24 Winter 2005 newsletter of Friends of the ABC (Victoria) http://www.fabc.org.au/vic/ [viewed12 July 2005].

25 Caitlin Moran paraphrasing BBC Three Controller Stuart Murphy in 'Go on, make me laugh,' *The Times*, T2 section, 8 August 2005, p. 15.

26 Tony Moore, 'These babies stopped booming in 1975', *The Australian*,

20 February 1997.
27 Phil Graham, publisher of *The Washington Post* from the late 1940s to 1962.
28 Andrew Marr, *My Trade: a short history of British Jounalism*, 2004, Pan Books, p. 234.
29 Turkey: eFacts, an e-Government Information Strategy, Gov3 consultancy, London, February 2005.
30 Dan Milmo, 'Where radio meets mobiles in digital spectrum', *The Guardian*, 16 December 2004.
31 Kevin Howley, St James Encyclopedia of Pop Culture http://www.findarticles.com/p/articles/mi_g1epc/is_tov/ai_2419100276 [viewed 9 August 2005].
32 Darren Armstrong, 'Crowded airwaves full of nothing,' *Sydney Morning Herald*, Heckler column, 11 July 2005.
33 Current Issues Brief no. 24 2002–03, by Alex Tewes for the Australian Parliamentary Library, 'War in Iraq: Preliminary Defense and Reconstruction Costs', Table Four, Direct Military Costs of Iraq War.
34 Peter Preston quoting Downie in 'The bottom line is not the home of freedom,' *The Observer*, Business and Media section, 17 April 2005.
35 Jack Schofield, 'Hacks of all Trades', *The Guardian*, Life supplement, 22 July 2004.
36 Anna Fifield, 'Log on. And don't forget to leave a tip', *Financial Times*, 6 November 2004.
37 Howard French, 'Online Newspaper Shakes Up Korean Politics', *New York Times*, 6 March 2003.

Chapter Ten

1 *The Observer Magazine*, 17 October 2004, p. 33.
2 Leon Gettler, 'She'll be right: our bosses chill out', *Sydney Morning Herald*, 21 March 2005.
3 Bernard Salt, demographer, author and KPMG partner, phone interview, May 2005.
4 Natasha Cica, *The Age*, 27 April 2005.
5 You can read all the submissions at: <http://www.aph.gov.au/senate/committee/legcon_ctte/expats03/submissions/sublist.htm>.
6 Carol Williams, 'Cultural diversity reflected in the victims', *Sydney Morning Herald*, 12 July 2005.
7 M. Timberlake and D.A. Smith, Data Set 10 of the Globalisation

ENDNOTES

and World Cities Study Group (a network of 100 researchers based in Leicestershire, UK), 2002 http://www.lboro.ac.uk/gawc>, [viewed 9 August 2005].

8 K. O'Connor, 'Rethinking Globalisation and Urban Development: the fortunes of Second-Ranked cities', in *Globalisation and World Cities (GaWC) Research Bulletin* 118, http://www.lboro.ac.uk/gawc [viewed 9 August 2005].

9 Deruder and Taylor, 'The Cliquishness of World Cities', 2003, from *Globalisation and World Cities (GaWC) Research Bulletin* 113 http://www.lboro.ac.uk/gawc [date viewed].

10 Australian Demographic Statistics, 3 June 2005, <http://www.abs.gov.au/AUSSTATS/abs%40.nsf/mf/3101.0?OpenDocument> [viewed 9 August 2005].

11 Department of Education, Science and Training, *Submission To The Senate Legal And Constitutional References Committee Inquiry Into Australian Expatriates*, February, 2004, p. i.

12 Figure 5.31 'NET OVERSEAS MIGRATION COMPONENTS – Selected years(a)' published in, *2005 Year Book Australia: Population and International migration*, http://www.abs.gov.au/ausstats/abs@.nsf/94713ad445ff1425ca25682000192af2/0bd75000987b71a0ca256f7200832f19!OpenDocument [viewed17 August 2005].

13 Department of Education, Science and Training, *Submission To The Senate Legal And Constitutional References Committee Inquiry Into Australian Expatriates*, February, 2004, p. ii.

14 Department of Education, Science and Training, *Submission To The Senate Legal And Constitutional References Committee Inquiry Into Australian Expatriates*, February, 2004, p. 1.

15 Department of Education, Science and Training, *Submission To The Senate Legal And Constitutional References Committee Inquiry Into Australian Expatriates*, February, 2004, p. 3.

16 Department of Education, Science and Training, *Submission To The Senate Legal And Constitutional References Committee Inquiry Into Australian Expatriates*, February, 2004, pp. 33–34.

17 G. Hugo, D. Rudd and K. Harris, *Australia's Diaspora: It's Size, Nature and Policy Implications*, CEDA Information Paper No 80 2003, p. 44.

18 Tim Colebatch, 'Bleeding the Third World: our $5 billion-a-year skills windfall', *The Age*, 25 October 2005.

Chapter Eleven

1 The fact that Steve Hutchins needs a footnote is proof of my point. He is a low-profile Senator for NSW, from the Australian Labor Party.
He is a former union leader from the Unity faction of the right wing of the ALP. He achieved notoriety in receiving the backing of right-wing factional leaders to be listed at the top of the ALP's 2004 Senate ticket in NSW, ahead of the more well known and respected Senator John Faulkner, triggering a rare revolt against him from many of his own factional supporters.
2 Douglas Alexander (UK Minister of State), *Progressive Outlook*, 2003, p. 48.
3 Hazel Blears (UK Labour Government minister), 2005.
4 Harry Evans, 'Twice the waste, thrice the inaction,' *Sydney Morning Herald*, Opinion section, June 21, 2005.
5 Rachel Hills, 'Branch stacking and fame tracking: how to get ahead in Australian politics', www.vibewire.net, [viewed 11 June 2004].
6 Anthony Gottlieb, 'The town of the talk', New York survey, *The Economist*, 19 February 2005.
7 Tony Vermeer, 'The Green Machine', *Sunday Telegraph*, 4 April 2004.
8 Guardian ICM poll (UK), December 2004.
9 Richard Reeves, 'We should all become time lords', *New Statesman*, 31 July 2000.
10 John Wood, UK Trade Unions Congress New Media Officer, speaking at Institute for Public Policy Research, 12 November 2004.
11 Figure provided by the Australian Council of Trade Unions at their first 'Youth Conference', YWCA, October 2002.

Chapter Twelve

1 Quigley was a former teacher of President Bill Clinton at Georgetown University, as quoted by Clinton in his acceptance speech at the 1992 Democratic Convention, New York, reprinted in Bill Clinton, *My Life*, Arrow Books, UK, 2005, p. 421.
2 Debra Jopson and Kelly Burke, 'Red ink, ivory towers', *Sydney Morning Herald*, 14 May 2005.
3 Interview with Andy Hornby, Chief Executive of the retail division at HBOS, *The Guardian*, Business section, 19 February 2005.; www.vibewire.net [viewed 12 July 2005].

4   Mark Lawson, 'We are what we read', *The Guardian*, Comment section, 18 February 2005.

Chapter Thirteen

1   I first read of the term 'as if', in relation to a concept Christopher Hitchins refers to in his book, *Letters to a Young Contrarian*, Basic Books, Cambridge MA, 2001, p. 36. Hitchens is quoting Vaclav Havel.
2   Katharine Graham, *Personal History*, Phoenix Press, London, 1997, p. 63.
3   Paul Arden, *It's not how good you are, it's how good you want to be*, Phaidon Press, London, 2003, p. 57.
4   Grant Butler, 'Now is Opportunity Time', http://www.abn.org.au/newsletters/opportunitytime.htm [viewed 9 August 2005].
5   Bernard Salt, 'The Young Rich', *Business Review Weekly*, 16–22 September 2004.
6   John Higgins, 'Our mission is the make the UK a nation of innovation', *Computing* (UK), 2 June 2005, p. 6.
7   ACSSO, ASPA, BCA, Jobs Australia, DSF, Smith Family and ACTU, *A 2004 Budget Proposal*, ACOSS, p. 2.
8   Richard Florida, *The Rise of the Creative Class*, Pluto Press, Annandale, 2002, p. 5.
9   Stephanie Peatling, 'New working week could help us get a life', *Sydney Morning Herald*, 15 March 2005.
10 'Snooze centres', *Spark* (UK), edition 3, 2004, p. 20.
11 Excerpt from an internet chat room posting as past of www.vibewire.net's e-Festival April 2005.
12 'Education: New Economy, New Challenges, a paper by the OECD International Futures Program, December 1999, http://www1.oecd.org/sge/au/Highlights19.htm [viewed 9 August 2005].

Chapter Fourteen

1   Bob Debus, NSW Minister for the Environment, in a speech to the NSW Fabian Society, 18 May 2005.
2   The method of squeezing out your political opponents by stealing their ideas, agreeing with anything that 60 percent of voters agree with or adopting a middle road position that is so weak no one can be successful in targeting you politically for holding the view.

3 Robin May quoted in 'There is going to be no magic solution,' *The Observer* (UK), 'Turning the Tide' supplement, 26 June 2005.
4 ICM poll (UK) based on a sample of 1010 adults, conducted between 10 and 12 June 2005.
5 Michelle Grattan, *The Age*, 29 May 2004; Peter Warshall, editor of *Whole Earth*, in Kelly and Leyden, *What's Next*, p. 242.
6 Peter Warshall, editor of *Whole Earth*, in Kelly and Leyden, *What's Next*, p. 242.
7 P.J. Taylor, 'Creating sustainable world cities: Homo Geographicus, A geohistorical manifesto for cities', http://www.lboro.ac.uk/gawc/rb/rb107.html [viewed 9 August 2005].
8 Part of the same focus group discussed earlier in Part Three. http://futuresfoundation.org.au/content/view/69/69/ [viewed 9 August 2005].
9 Valora Washington, 'Where Do We Go From Here?', *The American Prospect*, 1 November 2004.
10 Adele Horin, 'Infants denied trusted schemes', *Sydney Morning Herald*, 14 March 2005.
11 Marcia K. Meyers and Janet C. Gormick, 'The European Model,' *The American Prospect Online*, 1 November 2004.
12 Vivienne Parry, 'Child of the future', *The Guardian*, BeFit supplement, 22 January 2005, p. 6.
13 'Thinner-diet-for-junk-food-ads', *Sydney Morning Herald*, 28 January 2005.

Conclusion

1 <http://www.shelleconomistprize.com/winners2004.html> [viewed 9 August 2005].
2 From the FAQ page on www.notgoodenough.org, http://www.notgoodenough.org/index.php?page=21&sid=bfad7559cdb03a4df6ee6c721b010dde [viewed 6 September 2005].
3 This follows the philosophy of the Jewish leader David Ben-Gurion who, when threatened by the British Government with the prospect of there being no Jewish state after World War II, said: 'We will fight the Nazis as if there was no White Paper and fight the White Paper as if there are no Nazis.'
4 *The Australian*, Editorial, February 1997.

Index

A Current Affair, 138
Abbey, Dr, Ruth, 150
ABC, xvi, 35, 134–37
    Fly TV, 134
    radio, 131, 136
Absolutely Fabulous (Ab Fab), 85
Access Economics, 194–5
active denial technology, 34
activism
    as therapy, 84
ACTU, 170–71, 193
Adelaide, xv, 144–5
Adelaide-isation, 145
Ahlert, Christian, 46, 48
AIDS, 7, 61
Air Namibia, 137
Allan, Col, 131
Allan, Percy, 87

Alexander, Shana, 76
All Ordinaries, 119
Alston, Richard, 143
Amazon.com, 45, 187
anti-Apartheid movement, 31
anti-terrorism, 33
ANZ, 121
Anzac Day, 4–5
apathetic, 29
Aristotle, 58
Armstrong, Darren, 137
Ash, Geoff, 164
Astroboy, 48
ATSIC, 191
Australia Bureau of Statistics, 93, 151
Australian Computer Society, 195
Australia Day, 72

Australian Democrats, 27, 29, 34, 163, 165
Australian Financial Review, 119
Australian Greens Party, 161, 162–5
Australian Idol, 180
Australian Industry Group, 193
Australia Institute, The, 61
Australian Labor Party, xii, 144, 163, 166, 186, 193
    Labor's Cancer Plan, 144
    Young Labor, 190
Australian Prudential Regulation Authority, 119
AYPAC (Australian Youth Policy Action Coalition), 178

Baby Boomers xi–xii, xiv–xvi, xviii, 4, 5, 8, 15, 18, 30, 36, 40, 48, 49, 57, 58, 62, 68, 82, 83, 84, 86, 87, 141, 166, 176, 183, 185, 189–90, 193, 211
    and economic rationalism, 87
    feminist activism, 72
    hypocrisy, 85, 88
    nomenklatura, 84
    property, 90–96
    social movements, 88
Batman, 51
BBC, 134–5
Beazley, Kim, 155, 186
Becker, Gene, 46
Bedazzler, 68
Beecher, Eric, 128
Big Brother, 180, 192
Big Government, 35
Biggins, Jonathan, 4
Bit Torrent, 43
Blackberry, 40, 46
Blair Government, 207
Blogging, 39, 44, 47, 141
blue-collar workers, 169
Boltong, Anna, 150

Bondi, 93
Boomer Credibility Gap, 80, 81
Bradshaw, Carrie, 38
Bezhnev, Leonid, 81
brain circulation, 151
brain drain, 154
Bridget Jones' Diary, 60
Brisbane, 93, 152
Broadband, 37, 137–9, 141
Brokaw, Tom, 4
Brown, Bob, 164
Buckingham, Jeremy, 164
Bush, George, 43
Business Council of Australia, 111, 193–4

Cabinet, the, 77
Canberra, 188
Capitalism, 26, 27, 49, 168
Captain Corelli's Mandolin, 44
Career Kangaroos, 61, 63, 194
Carlton, Mike, 135
Carn, Scott, 9, 59
Carnegie, Andrew, 124
Carpenter, Gwen, 46
Carr, Bob, 96
Carrie Bradshaw, 35
Catholicism
    Catholic Church, 29
    school system, xiii
    Catholics, 29
Cavalier, Rodney, 155
Channel Four (UK), 134
Channel Nine, 130
Channel Seven, 133, 149
chat rooms, 47
Chesher, Chris, 57
China, 26
    Chinese people, 40
Challengers (The), 34
Childhood development, 207–9
Churchill, Winston, 155

INDEX

Cica, Natasha, 147
Cirque du Soleil, 124
Citibank, 126–7
citizenship education, 33, 189, 196–9
citizen reporters, 39
Clarke, Jane, 61
Clinton, Bill, 114
Clovelly, 93
Coalition, see Howard Government
Coffs Harbour, xiv, 103, 131
collective action, 47
Comedy Company, The, 28
Commonwealth Bank, 121, 197
community, xvii
Coollangatta, 144
corporate constitution, 120–1
Corporate Governance, 115, 117–19
Corporate Social Responsibility, 77, 114–15, 123–5
Costello, Peter, xvi, 193
   Inter-Generational Report, 100
Cox, Eva, 87
Creative Commons, 130
Crikey, 141
Cultural change, 175
Curie, Marie, 174

Daily Telegraph (Sydney), xiv, 131
Davis, Professor Glyn, 97
Davis, Mark, 87, 110
D-Day, 4
Degrassi, 51
deference, 37
de Hennin, Steve, 149
democracy, 166
   Big Brother style, 72
   in corporations, 120
   liberal, 26, 181
demographics, xii, xvi
Department of Education, Science and Training (DEST), 151
Desperate Housewives, 37

dole bludger, 63
diaspora, Australia, 56, 151
digital technology, 43
Discovering Democracy, 197
diversity, 8–11, 194
Donahoo, Daniel, 7
Dotcom boom, 124, 187
Downie, Len, 139
drugs,
   illegal, 6
   party, 73
Drysdale, Denise, 52
Duggan, Tim, 9, 41
Dusseldorp Skills Forum, 193–4
DVD, 41

eBay, 42, 44, 45, 47, 125
Ebbers, Bernie, 117
e-Commerce, 41
Economist, The
   on house prices, 77
   on cheap credit, 77
   on property binges, 92
   on immigration, 162
egalitarianism, 179
Einstein, Albert, 177
Elections
   2001 Federal, 144
   2004 Queensland, 164
Ellesmore, Sylvie, 34
elites, 176
email, 39
Emmerdale, 149
emigration, 151–5
Environment (the), 26, 201–3, 213
Epstein, Raphael, 136
equal pay, 121–2
   US, 122
   Italy, 122
ethical consumption, 33
Evans, Harry, 159
executive pay, 121

Fairfax, 139
fair go, 179
Faddoul, Daney, 103
Far Eastern Economic Review, 140
Fashion Week, Australian, 77, 146
Feminism, 41, 86
    second wave, 86
Fiorina, Carly, 116
First Home Owners Grant, 204
Fly TV, see ABC
Fonda, Jane, 64
Fong, Paula, 53, 65–6, 99
Forrest Gump, 87
Four Corners, 132, 136
Fox, Jo, 147
Freeman, Cathy, 197
Friends of the ABC, xiv, 135
Friends, 52
friendship networks, 57, 58
Freedom Ride, 1965, 35

Gallipoli, 5, 211
Gangland, 87
Garrett, Peter, 161
Gates, Bill, 40
Generations
    Generation eXpat, 143–54
    Generation HECS, 98–113
    Generation Jones, 8
    Generation Next, xi, 9
    Generation Text, 44
    Generation X, 4, 8, 9, 65, 90
    Generation Y, xii, xvi, 8, 9, 90
    Greatest Generation, 4
    handovers, 176
    labels, 7, 9
    length of, 3
    Millenials, 9
    The Challengers, 37
getup.org.au, 178
Gitlin, Todd, 31

Globalisation, xii, 23, 144, 206
    anti-corporate, 30, 48
Glue Issues, 200–9
Gold Coast Bulletin, 109
gold dusting, 64
Good Company, 29
Goodlass, Ray, 164
Google, 69
Governor-General, 72
GPS (Global Positioning System), 46
Grayling, Professor A.C., 76
Green, Antony, 165
Greens party, see Australian Greens
Greer, Germaine, 60, 148
Grey Power, 80, 189
Griffith Review, 57
'Growing Up Fast', 38
GST, 34, 163
Guardian, The, 48

Handshin, Mia, 130
Handy, Charles, 120–1
Harley, Jonathan, 136
Hawke, Bob, 36, 155, 212
HECS (Higher Education Contribution Scheme), 25, 98–113, 213
Hello Kitty, 51
Henderson, Brian, 133
Henry, Ken, xi
Herald Sun, 120
Herter, Andreas, 44
Hewlett Packard, 46
Hierarchies, 65
High Court, 160
HIH
    collapse of, 120
Hilton bombing, 1978, 33
Hilton, Paris, 130,
Hills, Rachel, 87, 180
Hitchens, Christopher, 79

INDEX

Holmes, Sam, 149
Horin, Adele, 96, 97, 107
House of Lords, 159
Housing 89–96, 111, 203–7
Howard Government, 151, 160, 166, 200
Howard, John, 28, 49, 155, 169, 184, 186, 202
Howard, Sean, 187
Hurricane Katrina, 55
Hutchins, Senator Steve, 155

IBM, 38
idealistic, 29
Iemma, Morris, 96
Imagining Australia, 179
individual contracts, 171
Industrial Relations Commission, 122
Industrial Revolution, 187
Information Revolution, 177
Informed consumption, 116
Ingold, Tammy, 86
innovation, 84, 123, 183, 186–96, 213
   and democracy, 188
   in design, 206
     National Office of the Innovation Economy, 188
International Year of Youth, 35
International Young Professionals Foundation, 63, 177
Internet, The, 27, 39, 42, 43, 45, 48
iGeneration, xvi
IKEA, xvi
iPod, xvi, 41, 161
Iraq
   Anti-war protests, 5, 28, 30

James, Clive, 148
Jellie, Bob, 77, 89
JJJ, see Triple J
job snob, 63

Johannesburg, 152
Jones, Alan, 137
Journalism,
   Australian, 8
   Business, 119
   criticism of, 131
   investigative, 139

Kaiser Chiefs, the, 6
Kasaniemi, Eija-Liisa, 44
Kath and Kim, 51, 85
Keating, Paul, 36, 212
Kennett, Jeff, 162
Kensington (Sydney), 27
Kernot, Cheryl, 125
King, Carole, 48
Kingston, Margo, 140
Klein, Naomi, 26
Knight, Dominic, 92
Knightley, Phillip, 132
Koutsikos, Kerry, 150
Kyoto Protocol, 114, 202
Kyriacou, Daniel, 106

lastminute.com, 187
Latham, Mark, 156, 186
Lawrence, Carmen, 192
Laws, John, 13
Lee, Warren 27
Legislation,
   limits of, 192
Left, the, xvii, 155, 162, 180
Lemaire, Alexis, xv
Lenin, V, 181
Lewis, Erica, 85–7, 106
libel laws, 138
Liberal Party, 168
Lions
   Clubs, 58
   Youth of The Year competition, 5
Lip, 178

Little Britain, 51, 90
Live Aid, 30
Live8, 30
Livingstone, Ken, 205
lobbying, 193
London
    terrorist bombings, 37
    the city, xv, 78, 131, 143, 152
    Underground, 39
Lyneham, Paul, 135
Lyons, Holly, 149

Macfarlane, Ian, 115
Mackenzie, Kenneth Scott, 112
Macquarie Bank, 134
Madden, David, 179
Main, Moira, 93
malodorant balls, 34
managers
    good, 66
    bad, 66
Mandela, Nelson, 174
Manly Youth Council, 60
Marles, Richard, 171
Marr, Andrew, 135
Mascot, 93
mateship, 179
Matson, Murray, 165
Mayer, Fredico, 97
Mayne, Stephen, 120
McAllister, Jenny, 144
McCartney, Paul, 2
McDonald, Geoff, 136
McPhee, Hilary, 61
McMansions, 91
Medicare, 203–04
mediocrity, xii
Melbourne, 77, 145, 152
Melbourne University, see
    University of Melbourne
Member/s of Parliament, 32, 49
metrosexuals, 60

Microsoft, 130,
Mierisch, Emily, 133, 137, 146
Miller, Lisa, 136
Minogue, Kylie, 147
Mitchell, Radha, 142
mobile phones, 45
More4 (UK TV channel), 134
Moss, Simon, 9, 34, 40, 63, 133, 176
Motion Picture Association of
    America, 44
Motorola, 44
moveon, 178
Mulgan, Geoff, 125
multi-channeling, 135, 138
Multiculturalism
    as an eating strategy, 85
multinationals, 35
multi-tasking, xvii
Murdoch, Rupert, 47, 107
Muslims, 131, 197
Mysterious Cities of Gold, The, 51

Nader, Ralph, 116
Napster, 43
National Australia Bank trading
    affair, 119
nationalisation, 169
National Union of Students (NUS),
    48
National Centre for Social and
    Economic Modelling (NATSEM),
    90, 111
national service, 198
National Youth Roundtable, 178
National Youth Transition Service
    (proposed), 193
negative gearing, 91
Negus, George, 135
Neil, Cameron, 55, 63
Nelson Review (of Australian
    Higher Education), 111
Nettle, Senator Kerry, 165

INDEX

Neville, Richard, 13, 88, 148, 175
New Journalism, 130
New Mardi Gras, 190, 191
News Limited, 119, 131, 139
New Matilda, 131
New Scientist, 60
New Statesman, 91
Newton, Bert, 133
New York, 78, 152, 162
New Zealand, 154
Nike, 48, 114
Nin, Anais, 3
Nine to Five, 64
Nobel Prize, xv
Noffs, Ted, 35
No Logo, 48
non-financial accounting, 115, 123
non-Government organisations, 161
nostalgia industry, 69
notgoodenough.org, 116, 177
NSW Property Council, 95

Oaktree Foundation (The), 34, 178
obesity, 195, 209
O'Brien, Kerry, 135
OECD
    on corporate governance, 118
    on education, 199
    on immigration, 153
O'Hara, Mary, 2
OhMyNews.com, 139–40
old age pensioner (OAP), 80
old boys networks, 150
O'Keefe, Claudia, 210
Oliver, Emma, 149
Oliver Twist, 72
Olympic Games, xv
Omidyar, Pierre, 45
One Nation, 165
OneTel,
    collapse of, 120, 187

Open Source Software, 130, 140
Oxford Internet Institute, 46
Oxford University, 125
OzEmail, 187
OzProspect (think tank), 7, 178

Paine, Tom, 84
Palagyi, Simon, 99
Paris, 152
Parliament,
    Australian, 157
    Dorothy Dixers, 157–8
Parton, Dolly, 64
Pasterfield Kate, 87
Patradoon, Sunita, 69
peer-to-peer networking, 43, 47, 130, 169
Perkins, Charles, 35
philanthropy, 115, 123–5
    Carnegie, 124
    Rockefeller, 124
Philip Morris (the company), 120
Play Power, 88
PlayStation, 40
Pocock, Barbara, 61
political correctness (PC), 71
politics
    advisers, 159, 166–7
    Aussie politicians, 157
    institutional, 156
    Whipped party system, 158, 159
popbitch, 52
Pope, the, 40, 181
Powerpoint, Microsoft, 69
Press Gallery
    Canberra, 138
Pressley, Alison, 102
Prime Minister, 32
Private Eye, 88
professional associations, 64
progress, xvii

Progressive
  politics, 162, 180
  young voters, 159
Property
  Property Apartheid, xvi, 80, 90, 93
  market, 84, 91
  speculation, 93
  taxes, 92
  vendor duty tax (NSW), 95
Protests
  peaceful, 33
  police at, 29
  protest control, 30
  street, 31
Prozac, 58
public education, 98–113
punctuation Nazis, 50
Putnam Robert, 46, 57

Qantas, 116
Quarterlife crisis, 21, 69
  rejection of, 69
Queer collaborations, 191
Queer Eye for the Straight Guy, 192
Quigley, Professor Carroll, 174

Radio
  FM, 136
  talkback, 32
  Turkish, 136
Real Estate Institute, 111
ReconciliACTION, 34, 178
Red Nose Day, 124
refugees, 163, 198
regulation, 117
Religion, 28
Right, The, 155, 180
Rio de Janiero, 152
Robinson, Jane, 131, 148
Ronald McDonald House, 124
Roosevelt, Theodore, 181

Rotary, 55
Rybak, Heidi, 150

safe sex, 61
Saffo, Paul, 65
Salt, Bernard, 53, 79, 144
Sampson, Annette, 95
Sao Paulo, 152
Sara, Sally, 136
scalability, 66
schoolfriends.com.au, 169
Schultz, Julianne, 132
Scissor Sisters, 37
Scouting groups, 59
Seachange, 89
seachange, 91
Secret Life of Us, The, 52, 57
Senate, Australian
  The Senate, 148, 159
  Senators, 32
Sex and the City, 38, 52, 60, 61
Shell, 114
Shop, Distributive and Allied Employees Union (SDA), 171
Simpsons, The, 52
Singletons, 60
skilled workers, 119, 151, 169
skills shortages, 143
Skoll, Jeff, 125
Sky News, 39
Skype, 27
Smith Family, The, 193
SMS, see text messaging
social capital, 46
social enterprise, 115, 123–5
social justice, 162
socialism, 169
social solidarity, 212
Sophocles, 213
Soviet Union, 81
Spanish Civil War, 44
Spanish Government, 50

INDEX

Spigelman, Jim, 35
Starsky and Hutch, 51
State Government bankruptcies, 34
Stateline, 132
Stewart, Fiona, 116, 211
Stoneham, Lisa, 112
Stott-Despoja, Natasha, 156, 161, 198
Street protests, 28
strikes, 169
Stu, 178
student activism, 102–4
Student protest, 29
Somers, Daryl, 52
Southern Cross Group, 55
Stock Exchange, Australian, 120
suburbia, 152
Summers, Anne, xiv, 32
Sun Herald, 60
Sunday Telegraph, 131, 164
superannuation, 204
Surry Hills, 162
Sustainable/sustainability, 7, 26, 27
Sydney, 77, 93, 128, 145, 152
Sydney Institute, The, 143
Sydney Morning Herald, 4, 29, 92, 95, 130, 220
    smh.com.au, 140
Sydney University, see University of Sydney

TAFE, 166
Tanner, Lindsay, 46
Taylor, Matthew, 91
technology, 40, 41
Television
    Free-to-air, 132
    Digital, 43, 77, 133, 141
    Industry, 132–6, 148
Telstra, 141
texting, see text messaging

Text messaging, 41, 44, 70
The Australian, 130, 141, 214
The Bill, 52
The Courier Mail, 13
The Good Life, 85
The Office, 52
This Day Tonight, 135
time sovereignty, 168
Today Tonight, 138
Tokyo, 152
Tom, Emma, 130
Tonga, 154
Tracey, Rose, 109
Transformers, 51
transparency, 118
trade unions, 168–71, 192
travel
    cheap air travel, 71
Trinity School, Sydney, 30
Triple J, 132, 137
Truss, Lynne 50
trust, 25, 46
Truth (defunct newspaper), 132
Tschaut, Nicole, 109
Tsunami, South Asian, 40
Turnbull, Malcolm, 161

UNESCO, 97
Unions, see Trade Unions
United Nations, 153
    Millenium Development Goals, 176
University of Melbourne, 31, 97, 108
    Youth Research Centre, 109
University of New South Wales, 27
University of Sydney, 101
University of Technology, Sydney, 31, 100, 104
Urban tribes, 57
US Department of Homeland Security, 43

VCR, 41
Velvet Underground, 137
Vibewire Youth Services, 133, 178
Video Mash-ups, 46
Vietnam war, 29
Virtual communities, 41
Voluntary Student Unionism, 178
Voting, 32

Wagga Wagga, 164
Wannous, Rannia, 147
War on Terror, 177
Warren Lee, 29
Washington Post, 139
Waterfront dispute, 171
Water Rats, 148
Watters, Ethan, 57
Weekly, Rhys, 91
Wellman, Barry, 55
Wesley Mission Centre, 120
Western Samoa, 154
West Wing, 52

Wilczek, Frank, xv
Will and Grace, 52
Wood, Anna (ecstasy death), 6
work/life balance, 168, 209
World Bank, 154
world cities, 152–3
WorldCom, 117
World Vision, 29
World War II, 4
Wyn, Johanna, 109

Yahoogroups, 48
Yale, 114
Yen, 178
Yeoh, Angela, 196
Yeon-Ho, Oh, 140
Yeppies (Young Experimenting Perfection seekers), 70
York, Anna, 86
Youth, achievement, xv
Youth, spirit of, xvii
YWCA, 178